TECHMARES

TECHMARES

The World's Dumbest Computer Users

Timothy D. McLendon

Writers Club Press

San Jose New York Lincoln Shanghai

TECHMARES
The World's Dumbest Computer Users

Writers Club Press
an imprint of iUniverse, Inc.

For information address:
iUniverse, Inc.
5220 S. 16th St., Suite 200
Lincoln, NE 68512
www.iuniverse.com

ISBN: 0-595-23689-8

Printed in the United States of America

For my parents, who taught me how to walk...more than once.
For Rose, the most beautiful and delicate flower.
For tech support workers all over the world; I feel your pain.

"I feel so much better now…just like taking a big poop…"

—www.techhell.com

CONTENTS

LIST OF CONTRIBUTORS

Contributing websites and their corresponding names in this publication include:

http://home.hvc.rr.com/nightowl2/index.html
NightOwl

http://www.techhell.com
Techhell

http://rinkworks.com/stupid
RinkWorks

http://www.idiotwatchers.com
Idiot Watchers

http://www.harryc.com
HarryC

http://www.unwind.com/jokes-funnies/computerjokes.shtml
Unwind

http://www.humorshack.com/archive/jokes/computer/index.shtml
HumorShack

http://www.shadowstorm.com/tech_support
ShadowStorm

http://www.monster-island.org/tinashumor/computer.html
Tina's Humor

http://www.netspace.org/~dmacks/internet-songbook/phone-callin.html
Daniel Macks

http://www.funny2.com/computer.htm
Funny2

http://www.seerialmom.com/
Seerialmom

http://www.yuckitup.com/tech.shtml
Yuckitup

http://www.cubiclecommando.com/jokes/techie/
Cubicle Commando

http://www.funny2.com/computer.htm
Funny2

http://www.siliconglen.com/jokes/contents.html
SiliconGlen

http://www.compguystechweb.com/humor/index.html
CompGuys

INTRODUCTION

Over the past two years I've witnessed some of the most horrific phone calls a computer technician could possibly handle. One female caller kept escalating through the ranks because she firmly believed that her laptop computer was causing radiation to her son's genitals. They don't train you to deal with situations like that. Another woman had to wear rubber gloves in order to use her computer; whenever she touched it with her bare hands it would immediately shut off. That brings a whole new meaning to electromagnetic interference. My favorite one was apparently a hacker issue. An older couple had a computer that told them it was sick and needed some fresh air. They ended up putting the computer on the back of their pickup truck and riding around the neighborhood fourteen times at 5 miles an hour with the emergency lights flashing. I'm sure the computer's feeling much better now.

I've been collecting stories like these that I've personally witnessed for quite some time. The purpose, of course, was to put them together for a book. Unfortunately, I was met with a stark realization not too long ago. I couldn't come up with enough material for a twenty-page thriller and God only knows how long it would take for enough stupid people to leave their indelible mark in my life.

That's when the real quest began. I scoured the Internet for the funniest tech support stories I could find. It was then that I ran into another roadblock. The same stories appeared over and over on nearly every website dealing with this subject! Ack. Another quest was born after weeks of witnessing this massacre. I had to find not only the funniest stories but also the most original stories and jokes available, which means I had to build a relationship with the authors. It wasn't an easy feat but everyone's been great. You may recognize many of these, and I apologize, but many of them you will not.

All of the websites presented offer standard legal disclaimers, as do I. Some of these stories and jokes are not original and have been around for many years, released into the public domain. Every attempt was made to contact the original authors. If you believe anything presented here is your original work then please contact me so that I make update this information in future publications.

I originally thought this would be the easiest thing in the world and I'd have this book done in a matter of weeks and in my spare time. I'll tell you this much…that spare time turned out to be between four and eight hours a day, everyday of the week. Hours turned into days, days turned into weeks, weeks turned into months. I don't regret one minute of it though. If one person laughs after reading this book then I've accomplished what I'm after.

Timothy D. McLendon
tim_mclendon@hotmail.com

THE FIRST SIGN OF TROUBLE

Troubleshooting skills have been important since the beginning of time. With or without computers, people have always been dumb. And so the saga began…

"Fire help. Me Grog."

"Me Lorto. Help. Fire not work."

"You have flint and stone?"

"Ugh."

"You hit them together?"

"Ugh."

"What happen?"

"Fire not work."

"[sigh] Make spark?"

"No spark, no fire. Me confused. Fire work yesterday."

"[sigh] You change rock?"

"I change nothing."

"You sure?"

"Me only make little change. Stone hot so me soak in stream so stone not burn Lorto's hand. Only small change, shouldn't keep Lorto from make fire."

Grog grabs club and goes to Lorto's cave, "fixes" problem.

—*HarryC*

Fast forward to modern day...

Husband: Wife! Children! Get in the car. We're gonna buy a computer.
Children: Yaaaayy!
Wife: But Husband, we don't know anything about computers. Shouldn't we at least buy a magazine or something? Maybe learn something before we spend our money?
Husband: Nonsense, Wife. Nothing I can't handle. Just let me do the talking.

Cut to the "Mass Market Computer Store"

Entry Level Clerk: Hello, how can I help you?
Husband: We want a computer. *(Picks one at random)* Tell me about this one?
Entry Level Clerk: That's a really, really, REALLY good one.
Husband: How many RAMS does it have?
Entry Level Clerk: Well...ummm...*(reading from box)* it has 256 MEGS OF RAM!
Husband: That's good, right?
Entry Level Clerk: Of course. Think about it. It's TWICE as good as 128 megs.
Husband: Wow–good point. Does it have that there Internet in it?
Entry Level Clerk: Oh yes. The whole Internet is right inside there.
Husband: Boy, you really know your stuff. I'll take it.
Our hero, the clerk: *(Muttering under his breath)* Whew! Dodged another one.
Wife: What about tech support? *(hubby growls)* Not that we'll need it. *(Nice recovery)*
Mr. Entry Level: Oh, Tech Support is included. If you ever have any trouble, just call them and they will solve all of your problems. Tech Support will help you recover from any disaster, even the ones you cause. Tech support means never having to worry about learning how to use this machine. If people are mean to you, Tech Support will kill them. Tech support is every person's dream come true.

—NightOwl

...to be continued...

Let me interrupt this story just briefly. Salesmen. They tell you whatever you want to hear. I hate them. Every last one of them. They may have their own high-tech computer sales jargon, but they don't know jack about computers:

New: Different color from previous design.

All New: Parts not interchangeable with previous design.

Exclusive: Imported product.

Unmatched: Almost as good as the competition.

Designed simplicity: Manufacturer's cost cut to the bone.

Foolproof operation: No provision for adjustments.

Advanced design: The advertising agency doesn't understand it.

It's here at last!: Rush job; Nobody knew it was coming.

Field-tested: Manufacturer lacks test equipment.

High accuracy: Unit on which all parts fit.

Direct sales only: Factory had big argument with distributor.

Years of development: We finally got one that works.

Revolutionary: It's different from our competitors.

Breakthrough: We finally figured out a way to sell it.

Futuristic: No other reason why it looks the way it does.

Distinctive: A different shape and color than the others.

Maintenance-free: Impossible to fix.

Redesigned: Previous faults corrected, we hope...

Hand crafted: Assembly machines operated without gloves on.

Performance proven: Will operate through the warranty period.

Meets all standards: Ours, not yours.

All solid state: Heavy as Hell!

Broadcast quality: Gives a picture and produces noise.

High reliability: We made it work long enough to ship it.

SMPTE bus compatible: When completed, will be shipped by Greyhound.

New generation: Old design failed, maybe this one will work.

Mil-spec components: We got a good deal at a government auction.

Customer service across the country: You can return it from most airports.
Unprecedented performance: Nothing we ever had before worked this way.
Built to precision tolerance: We finally got it to fit together.
Satisfaction guarantee: Manufacturer's, upon cashing your check.
Microprocessor controlled: Does things we can't explain.
Latest aerospace technology: One of our techs was laid off by Boeing.

—*Tina's Humor Archive*

...thank you for your patience...the story continues...

So, the computer makes it home, and the father gets right to it. I will now switch gears, and present the rest of the story in chronological order:

2:00pm Father tears open the box, and promptly crumples up the paper that says "Read me first". He throws it away. He finds the owner's manual. It gets put in the bottom drawer, never to see daylight again.
2:12pm He reaches into the garbage pail, realizing that paper tells him where to put "all those wires".
2:27pm Wonders why a "stupid warehouse person" included a phone cord in the box.
2:47pm After three re-wires, the computer comes to life.
3:37pm After pressing "delete" at startup 12 times (the screen said to), he gets to "Windows 98" with only minimal damage to his configurations.
3:39pm Clicks "American Online" icon–is greeted with "no dialtone".
3:40pm Calls Tech Support.
3:42pm Hangs up after holding for "over 15 minutes".
3:43pm Redials–holds for "well over 30 minutes". Hangs up just before I answer.
3:48pm Redials–back to the end of the line. Puts it on speakerphone.
3:52pm I answer. Father screams at me, saying he's been on hold for "over an hour". I look for a hard surface to bang my head against. I'll probably be needing it.

4:03pm After listening to the tirade, and how he paid "two thousand dollars" (MSRP $1,200) for this machine, I get him to tell me what his problem is. I ask him to click on Start. He replies "Oh, the computer has to be on?"

4:05pm Computer finishes booting back up.

4:06pm I ask him if the modem is plugged in. He says it is–there's stuff on the screen.

4:10pm He finally understands that the modem is INSIDE the computer. Insists it's plugged in.

4:10pm I ask him to "right click" on the My Computer icon.

4:11pm Asks me "How the hell am I supposed to WRITE the word "click" on YOUR computer." The wall of the cubicle will have to do.

4:22pm Finally in device manager. All settings seem ok. I ask him to double check the phone cord he insisted was plugged in. "What phone cord?" he says. I mute and sob.

4:29pm Insists it didn't come with a phone cord or owner's manual. And for "twenty five hundred dollars" (MSRP $1,200) it damn well should have.

4:38pm Finds the phone cord. Two feet short for his setup. Insists he cannot move the desk.

4:40pm Screams that for "three thousand dollars" (MSRP $1,200), it should come with a longer cord.

4:41pm Insists I "send someone out" to hook this "phone thing up".

4:49pm Moves the desk two feet. Surprisingly, the house doesn't tilt.

4:55pm He dials on "American Online" before I tell him to, thankfully cutting us off.

5:05pm Calls back. Why should he have to put his credit card # in. After all, he's already paid "thirty five hundred dollars" (MSRP $1,200).

5:15pm After explaining free enterprise to him, he asks me to recommend a book on computers. I tell him the owner's manual is rather informative. I also convince him that there really is a book entitled "Windows for complete and utter morons".

—*Night Owl*

The average consumer has no idea how much stress is involved in fielding phone calls from the technically deficient public. Anyone who has ever spent time working in tech support will verify that the challenge is somewhat similar to that of an air traffic controller. The stress level could be completely reduced with one little change…the phone routing system…

Ring…Ring…Ring…Ring…Ring…Ring…Ring…Ring…Ring…Ring…
Ring…Ring…Ring…Ring…Ring…Ring…Ring…Ring…Ring…Ring…
Ring…Ring…Ring…Ring…Ring…Ring…Ring…Ring…Ring…Ring…
Ring…Ring…

Thank you for calling Technical Support. All of our technicians are currently busy helping people who are even less competent than you, so please hold for the next available technician. The waiting time is now estimated at between fifteen minutes and eternity.

In order to expedite your call, please punch your 58-digit product identification number onto your telephone, followed by your product serial number, which can be found in a secret compartment inside your computer where, for security purposes, it is printed in the smallest typeface possible to prevent being seen. Please note that you may need a size 11 3/4 torx screwdriver, which may only be available from your original equipment manufacturer.

Do that NOW!

Thank you again for calling Technical Support. We recommend that you sit at your computer, preferably turning it on at some point, and have at hand all your floppy disks, CD-ROM disks, computer manuals and original packing materials in order to allow the technician to aid you in the unlikely event that he ever gets to your call.

If you were an inconsiderate jerk—we mean forgetful customer—and threw away your original packing materials, please call the company that sent you the computer and ask them to resend you the empty box with the plastic bubbles, fake popcorn and the wasted paper advertising that they recycle. We will hold your place in line on the phone while you wait for your boxes to be delivered. (yeah right!)

It would also be helpful for you to refrain from sobbing while explaining your problem to the technician. Shouting obscene threats will cause you to be immediately disconnected and blackballed from further communication with Technical Support, not only from ours but that of every other electronics-related firm in the industrialized world. (We all talk, you know)…

Thank you once again for calling Technical Support. In order to enable us to better assist you, it would be helpful to know more about you and your equipment. Have you called Technical Support before? If you have, please press the numeral "one" on your telephone touch pad.

If not, press the numeral "two." If you are not sure, using the letters on your touch pad, spell out the phrase: "I am confused and despondent and quickly losing the will to live." Once you have finished, hang up your phone and make arrangements to sell your computer because by the time the technician takes your call, it will be obsolete, and you will be too senile to use it anyway.

Thank you for calling Technical Support. Unfortunately, all of our technicians just went out for lunch. This means that to the estimated waiting time we gave you earlier, you may now add at least another two hours.

Thank you for calling Technical Support. Before talking to the technician about your problem and risking the possibility that you may be wasting his valuable time, please ask yourself the following questions:

1. If my monitor screen is dark, is it possible I have forgotten to plug in my computer?
2. Have I exhausted every possible means of help before utilizing the sacred, last-resort-only telephone option?
3. Have I sent a fax to Fast Fax Technical Support?
4. Have I consulted my manual?
5. Have I read the Read-Me notice on the floppy disk?
6. Have I called up my know-it-all geek cousin who I can't stand but who can probably fix this thing for me in under five minutes?
7. Have I given the central processing unit of my computer a good, solid whack?

If you cannot honestly answer "yes" to all these questions, please get off the line immediately so that our overworked technicians can help those truly desperate customers whose suffering is so much greater than yours. You must be really bored that you have to call Technical Support just to have someone to speak to about geek stuff…

Thank you for calling Technical Support. You may not be aware that this week we are featuring a discount on a number of popular CD-ROM titles you may wish to purchase, such as the best-selling Porn Doubler, which allows you to access erotic material from the Internet twice as fast. If you would like to hear all 26,000 titles read to you, shout "Yes! Yes! Yes!" into the telephone now. This will not cause you to lose your place in line for Technical Support; in fact it may jump you ahead of several other callers.

Thank you for calling Technical Support. Our System has been over-loaded, and unfortunately you have lost your place in line. Please push "one" if you would like to be connected again to Technical Support.

Thank you for calling Technical Support. Our electronic sensors indicate that you are about to slump over and die from a massive frustration attack combined with severe dehydration from lack of food and water. Before doing so, please take a moment to place your telephone receiver back in its base and switch off your computer so as not to wear down its internal battery.

As a non-living person, you will have no further need of Technical Support and so we regretfully must remove you from our list of registered product users.

Remember, we valued your patronage and were happy to serve your needs. Do not hesitate to have your heirs or beneficiaries contact us should any further technical problems arise.

—*HarryC*

Poor bastard. The first hurdle for a phone technician is overcoming any language barrier there may be with the customer. This isn't always as easy as it sounds…

The Nine Types Of Users

El Explicito–"I tried the thing, ya know, and it worked, ya know, but now it doesn't, ya know?"
Advantages: Provides interesting communication challenges.
Disadvantages: So do chimps.
Symptoms: Complete inability to use proper nouns.
Real Case: One user walked up to a certain Armenian pod manager and said, "I can't get what I want!" The pod manager leaned back, put his hands on his belt-buckle, and said, "Well, ma'am, you've come to the right place."

Mad Bomber–"Well, I hit ALT-f6, shift-f8, CNTRL-f10, f4, and f9, and now it looks all weird."
Advantages: Will try to find own solution to problems.
Disadvantages: User might have translated document to Navajo without meaning to.
Symptoms: More than six stopped jobs in 'UNIX', a 2:1 code-to-letter ratio in 'WordPerfect'.
Real Case: One user came in complaining that his WordPerfect document was underlined. When I used reveal codes on it, I found that he'd set and unset underline more than fifty times in his document.

Frying Pan/Fire Tactician–"It didn't work with the data set we had, so I fed in my aunt's recipe for key lime pie."
Advantages: Will usually fix error.
Disadvantages: 'Fix' is defined VERY loosely here.
Symptoms: A tendency to delete lines that get errors instead of fixing them.
Real Case: One user complained that their program executed, but didn't do anything. The scon looked at it for twenty minutes before realizing that they'd commented out EVERY LINE. The user said, "Well, that was the only way I could get it to compile."

Shaman–"Last week, when the moon was full, the clouds were thick, and formahaut was above the horizon, I typed f77, and lo, it did compile."
Advantages: Gives insight into primitive mythology.
Disadvantages: Few scon are anthropology majors.
Symptoms: Frequent questions about irrelevant objects.
Real Case: One user complained that all information on one of their disks got erased (as 'Norton Utilities' showed nothing but empty sectors, I suspect nothing had ever been on it). Reasoning that the deleted information went *somewhere*, they wouldn't shut up until the scon checked four different disks for the missing information.

X-user–"Will you look at those…um, that resolution, quite impressive, really."
Advantages: Using the cutting-edge in graphics technology.
Disadvantages: Has little or no idea how to use the cutting-edge in graphics technology.
Symptoms: Fuzzy hands, blindness.
Real Case: When I was off duty, two users sat down in front of me at DEC station 5000/200s systems that were reconfiguring. I suppressed my laughter while, for twenty minutes, they sat down and did their best to act like they were doing exactly what they wanted to do, even though they couldn't log in.

Miracle Worker–"But it read a file from it yesterday!" 'Sir, at a guess, this disk has been swallowed and regurgitated.' "But I did that a month ago, and it read a file from it yesterday!"
Advantages: Apparently has remarkable luck when you aren't around.
Disadvantages: People complain when scon actually use the word 'horse-puckey'.
Symptoms: Loses all ability to do impossible when you're around. Must be the kryptonite in your pocket.
Real Case: At least three users have claimed that they've loaded 'IBM WordPerfect' from 'Macintosh' disks.

Taskmaster–"Well, this is a file in 'MacWrite'. Do you know how I can upload it to 'MUSIC', transfer it over to 'UNIX' from there, download it onto an 'IBM', convert it to 'WordPerfect', and put it in three-column format?"
Advantages: Bold new challenges.
Disadvantages: Makes one wish to be a garbage collector.
Symptoms: An inability to keep quiet. Strong tendencies to make machines do things they don't want to do.
Real Case: One user tried to get a scon to find out what another person's E-mail address was even though the user didn't know his target's home system, account name, or real name.

Maestro–"Well, first I sat down, like this. Then I logged on, like this, and after that, I typed in my password, like this, and after that I edited my file, like this, and after that I went to this line here, like this, and after that I picked my nose, like this."
Advantages: Willing to show you exactly what they did to get an error.
Disadvantages: For as long as five or six hours.
Symptoms: Selective deafness to the phrases, "Right, right, okay, but what was the ERROR?" and a strong fondness for the phrase, "Well, I'm getting to that."
Real Case: I once had to spend half an hour looking over a user's shoulder while they continuously retrieved a document into itself and denied that they did it (the user was complaining that their document was 87 copies of the same thing).

Princess (unfair, perhaps, as these tend, overwhelmingly, to be males) "I need a 'Mac', and someone's got the one I like reserved, would you please garrote him and put him in the paper recycling bin?"
Advantages: Flatters you with their high standards for your service.
Disadvantages: Impresses you with their obliviousness to other people on this planet.
Symptoms: Inability to communicate except by complaining.
Real Case: One asked a scon to remove the message of the day because he (the user) didn't like it.

Once the technician can decipher the customer's language, he must then coax the customer into describing the actual problem. This, also, is not as easy as it sounds. That's why most techs have a standard slew of questions to hammer the customer with. For example, take the following form...

Computer Problem Report Form

1. Describe your problem:

_____

_____

2. Now, describe the problem accurately:

_____

_____

3. Speculate wildly about the cause of the problem:

_____

_____

4. Problem Severity:
A. Minor__
B. Minor__
C. Minor__
D. Trivial__

5. Nature of the problem:
A. Locked Up__
B. Frozen__
C. Hung__
D. Strange Smell__

6. Is your computer plugged in? Yes__ No__

7. Is it turned on? Yes__ No__

8. Have you tried to fix it yourself? Yes__ No__

9. Have you made it worse? Yes__

10. Have you had a friend who knows all about computers that can try fix it for you? Yes__ No__

11. Did they make it even worse? Yes__

12. Have you read the manual? Yes__ No__

13. Are you sure you've read the manual? Maybe__ No__

14. Are you absolutely certain you've read the manual? No__

15. If you read the manual, do you think you understood it? Yes__ No__

16. If Yes, then explain why you can't fix the problem yourself.

_____

_____

17. What were you doing with your computer at the time the problem occurred?

_____

_____

18. If you answered nothing, then explain why you were logged in?

_____

_____

19. Are you sure you aren't imagining the problem? Yes__ No__

20. Does the clock on your home VCR blink 12:00? Yes__ What's a VCR?__

21. Do you have a copy of 'PCs for Dummies'? Yes__ No__

22. Do you have any independent witnesses to the problem? Yes__ No__

23. Do you have any electronics products that DO work? Yes__ No__

24. Is there anyone else you could blame this problem on? Yes__ No__

25. Have you given the machine a good whack on the top? Yes__ No__

26. Is the machine on fire? Yes__ Not Yet__

27. Can you do something else instead of bothering me? Yes__

—*HumorShack*

If you're an employee in a large company that incorporates helpdesk support, here are a few guidelines to enlighten your relationship with the helpdesk. Do you hear sarcasm?

1. When a tech says he's coming right over, log out and go for coffee. It's no problem for us to remember 2700 network passwords.

2. When you call us to have your computer moved, be sure to leave it buried under half a ton of postcards, baby pictures, stuffed animals, dried flowers, bowling trophies and 'Popsicle' art. We don't have a life and we find it deeply moving to catch a fleeting glimpse of yours.

3. When tech support sends you an e-mail with high importance, delete it at once. We're probably just testing out the public groups.

4. When a tech is eating lunch at his desk, walk right in and spill your guts out and expect him to respond immediately. We exist only to serve and are always ready to think about fixing computers.

5. When a tech is at the water cooler or outside having a smoke, ask him a computer question. The only reason why we drink water or smoke at all is to ferret out all those users who don't have email or a telephone line.

6. Send urgent email ALL IN UPPERCASE. The mail server picks it up and flags it as a rush delivery.

7. When you call a tech's direct line, press 5 to skip the bilingual greeting that says he's out of town for a week, record your message, and wait

exactly 24 hours before you send an email straight to the director because no one ever returned your call. You're entitled to common courtesy.

8. When the photocopier doesn't work, call computer support. There's electronics in it, right?

9. When you're getting a NO DIAL TONE message at home, call computer support. We can even fix telephone problems from here.

10. When something's wrong with your home PC, dump it on a tech's chair with no name, no phone number, and no description of the problem. We love a good mystery.

11. When you have a tech on the phone walking you through changing a setting—read the paper. We don't actually mean for you to DO anything; we just love to hear ourselves talk.

12. When we offer training on the upcoming OS upgrade, don't bother. We'll be there to hold your hand after it is done.

13. When the printer won't print, re-send the job at least 20 times. Print jobs frequently just disappear into the cosmos for no reason.

14. When the printer still won't print after 20 tries, send the job to all 68 printers in the office. One of them is bound to work.

15. Don't use online help. Online help is for wimps.

16. If you're taking night classes in computer science, feel free to go around and update the network drivers for you and all your co-workers. We're grateful for the overtime when we have to stay until 2:30am fixing them.

17. When you have a tech fixing your computer at a quarter past one, eat your lunch in his face. We function better when slightly dizzy.

18. Don't ever thank us. We love this AND we get paid for it!

19. When a tech asks you whether you've installed any new software on this computer, lie. It's nobody's business what you've got on your computer.

20. If the mouse cable keeps knocking down the framed picture of your dog, lift the computer and stuff the cable under it. Mouse cables were designed to have 45 lbs. of computer sitting on top of them.

21. If the space bar on your keyboard doesn't work, blame it on the mail upgrade. Keyboards work much better with half a pound of muffin crumbs, nail clippings, and big sticky drops of Coke under the keys.

22. When you get the message saying "Are you sure?" click on the Yes button as fast as you can. Hell, if you weren't sure, you wouldn't be doing it, would you?

23. Feel perfectly free to say things like "I don't know nothing about that computer crap". It never bothers us to hear our area of professional expertise referred to as crap.

24. When you need to change the toner cartridge, call tech support. Changing a toner cartridge is an extremely complex task, and Hewlett-Packard recommends that it be performed only by a professional engineer with a Master's degree in nuclear physics.

25. When something's the matter with your computer, ask your secretary to call the help desk. We enjoy the challenge of having to deal with a third party who doesn't know anything about the problem.

26. When you receive a 30-meg movie file, send it to everyone as a high-priority mail attachment. We've got plenty of disk space and processor capacity on that mail server.

27. Don't even think of breaking large print jobs down into smaller chunks. God forbid somebody else might get a chance to squeeze into the queue.

28. When you bump into a tech in the grocery store on a Saturday, ask a computer question. We work 24/7, even while at the grocery store on weekends.

29. If your son is a student in computer science, have him come in on the weekends and do his projects on your office computer. We'll be there

for you when his illegal copy of Visual Basic 6.0 makes your Access database flip out.

30. When you bring us your own no-brand home PC to repair for free at the office, tell us how urgently we need to fix it so your son can get back to playing TAK. We'll get right on it because we have so much free time at the office. Everybody knows all we do is surf the Internet all day anyway.

31. When you see an error message come up on your screen, delete it immediately without writing down the message. Techies would rather not know what's broke when they come to fix it.

I can't end this chapter without going back to the very beginning of time, and how this whole tech support mess started. Here's a history of the Ten Commandments of Tech Support Callers, presented by Virginia Gundel, a.k.a. Seerialmom:

In the beginning there was mainframe; and it was good.
On the second day Lord Jobs and Lord Wozniak gathered up the fruits of their humble abode and created Apple; the masses rejoiced at their new freedom.
On the third day the Almighty Bill created Microsoft; this caused the people to turn their backs on the Apple for they knew not what they did.
On the last day, the Ten Commandments were created in an attempt to redeem the souls of those peoples.
Here then, are those Ten Commandments:

1. Thou shalt knoweth the exact error and be prepared to recite it when prompted by thine Tech Support Personnel!

Maybe I have way too much common sense but calling Tech Support when you don't have the error message is like going to the doctor and saying "I have a pain" and when he asks "where?" you answer "In my body, somewhere". 'Nuff said.

2. Thou shalt not call Tech Support when thou hast not rested thy brain from the turmoil caused by thine operating system!

Why anyone in their right mind would keep hitting their head against the wall is beyond me. Personally, I walk away from the PC and do something else for a while if I'm not sure what the problem is. Likewise, before I even consider installing hardware or "major" software (like an operating system), I make sure I'm calm, cool and collected.

3. Thou shalt refrain from cursing at thy Tech Support when thou doth not agree with the diagnosis given by the aforementioned!

You know, swearing like a sailor or threatening the tech will not get your system fixed any faster. In fact, the tech may be so "shaken" by your tirade he may "inadvertently" give you the wrong instruction for your problem ("sir, I believe doing the following will solve your problem: exit out to the DOS prompt and type c:\fdisk").

4. Thou shalt not call Tech Support while under the influence of alcohol or any other mind altering substances!

Although we in Tech Support will probably chuckle for the first few minutes if you call in drunk, after that we tend to get annoyed. Playing games or "chatting" on the Internet are fine while intoxicated; running System Editor or the Registry Editor are not. Luckily for you, most decent techs will handle the situation by suggesting you call back later, when you've had about five less beers!

5. Thou shalt not call Tech Support unless thy PC is on and ye hath ample time to spend seeking the truth of thine problems!

Please do NOT call five minutes before leaving for work, or on your "coffee break". Calling us from work when your PC is crashed at home is futile; we can't begin to investigate the cause unless you're right there look-ing at the PC. Also, unless you're a true techno-whiz, our instructions will do nothing more than confuse you anyway. Last, have the PC on and ready to go BEFORE dialing the 800#, most of us are on some type of time con-straint and waiting for your 386SX to boot up is highly annoying.

6. Thou shalt not start thine call with "I'm computer illiterate"!

I'll make this as simple as possible. Please go back and read command-ment #II at the following site: http://seerialmom.homestead.com/files/10com.html. Besides that, we in tech support tend to assume you know nothing and 9 times out of 10 you prove us right.

7. Thou shalt not give thy Tech Support Personnel thy qualifications or present employment title!

If I had a nickel for every "System Administrator" or "Network Administrator" who called, I'd do a hostile takeover of Microsoft. Likewise, I nor any of my fellow techs are impressed when you proceed to give us your lofty title of Dr. anything. Come to think of it, the most obnoxious calls I've had came from these supposedly "intelligent" jerks.

8. Thou shalt listen to thy Tech Support Personnel and proceed not unless thou hath been instructed to do so!

Did you ever play "Simon Says" as a kid? Well, tech support is just like that and Simon will get very nasty with you if you close programs or windows he needs you to have open or click on things that have nothing to do with what we're trying to help you fix. Likewise, do NOT reset your PC just because you've got an "hourglass"; there are other ways to stop the program without trashing your operating system. If you'd quit jumping the gun we'll gladly tell you how to do it.

9. Thou shalt confess to thy Tech Support Personnel all sins committed against thine operating system!

When calling tech support, it's a good idea to know exactly what you've installed in the days prior to the problem occurring, even if you think it's not related. We especially need to know if you've installed any "utility" type program (can you say "First Aid"?). I realize these magic "utility" programs that promise to fix whatever ailments may beset your PC sound like a dream come true, but the reality is that more often than not, they cause more problems than they actually fix.

10. Thou shalt remove any or all distractions, for they will surely prevent ye from receiving the divine assistance ye art seeking!

Please don't call us when you're in the middle of an argument with your spouse, or when your two-year old is screaming at the top of his lungs. Also, turn down your TV or stereo and definitely do NOT call while you're having a party. One more thing; do not call us if your wife just said she's leaving you, your mind will definitely be someplace else, eh?

Editor's Note: Virginia Gudgel holds a BA in Psychology and is the single parent of two teens. Be sure to visit her website at http://www.seerialmom.com. Here are a few words from the author...

I started out by volunteering as "staff" for a local BBS/ISP (when the Internet first went commercial); advanced to working for a major ISP doing Tech Support. After that I progressed to server support for a dot-com and then on to my present position working in the Help Desk for the employees of a chip manufacturer.

Why did I start my website? I was doing tech support for the major ISP and after about two years I concluded there was a common thread to all new computer users and felt that my fellow techies would "relate" to the commonality and get a chuckle at the suggestions.

I've been in customer service almost my whole life; in relation to the customers I provide support for, I enjoy fixing their problems and especially like it when I've been able to ease their fears about technology.

Virginia

NIGHT OWL

I started my website when I was a computer tech because I noticed that every other "tech humor" website out there had the exact same stories. Every one had the "CD-ROM is a coffee holder" story, and I just thought there was so much more that needed to be said. Plus, it made me feel better to make fun of the idiots that called. Now, don't get me wrong, I don't *hate* all the callers, but I did develop a strong dislike for the ones that would call without ever opening the manual, or the idiots that would tell *me* how to fix it, or (even worse), the ones that believed their "computer expert" friend (who sells shoes for a living) over me. I ended up giving this friend a name on my website (he's the "Mel" I make fun of).

I ran my site for about three years and got quite the following in that time (I would say that at its time, my website was the most popular "tech" website out there). I still get a lot of mail regarding the site, even though I am no longer a tech. I left tech support for a job as an EDI mapper (e-commerce type programming), and still freelance EDI mapping today (I'm a freelance consultant). I also decided to leave the computer business altogether in a few years and be a teacher, so I am currently in school to get my teaching degree. Let's just say I'm tired of dealing with computer-illiterate idiots.

—*Dan Furman*

Editor's Note: Dan Furman Lives in Kingston, New York, and functions as a freelance computer consultant. He married his wife, Maryellen, 35 days after meeting her. Together, they own two stupid dogs. I like this guy.

Check out his website at: http://home.hvc.rr.com/nightowl2/index.html or send him an email at: nightowl@hvc.rr.com.

The following people will not get it or may be offended:

Those who call their computer "that box".
Those who call the monitor the computer.
Anyone who freezes when the mouse does.
Those without a sense of humor.
People whose IQ's hover around room temperature.
Anyone who takes things too seriously.

Feel my wrath, Mel

Owl: Tech Support. Can I help you?

Caller: Hey there–I've got my friend MEL on the line with us. He's a computer expert. He'll tell you what's wrong. You there, Mel?

Owl: Wait, hang on a sec. I have a few questions. So, Mel, are you that friend everyone has who's a "computer genius"?

Mel: Ummmm, yeah…I suppose.

Owl: But in reality, you know very little, right?

Mel: Ummm, uh…

Owl: And you make everything you touch worse. Correct?

Mel: Well, once I fixed the toaster, but that was…

Owl: And I can see how that qualifies you to work on computers. Mel, why do you do this? Do you think it will make you more attractive to women?

Mel: Well, I always wanted to be a computer guy–you guys are so cool–wait…"RAM, motherboard, hard drive" see–I can do it…

Owl: Mel, I think you should leave the computer stuff to me, and stick to selling shoes, ok?

Mel: How did you know I sold shoes?

Anyone for a threesome???

Owl: Tech Support, can I help you?

Caller: Hey there, I've got my friend MEL on the line with us. He's a computer expert. He'll tell youwhat's wrong. You there, Mel?

Mel: What?

Caller: Mel?

Mel: Yeah?

Caller: Go ahead.

Mel: With what?

Caller: Tell him what's wrong with the computer.

Mel: Tell who?

Caller: The tech...

Mel: The tech is at your house?

Owl: Mel, it's a three way call. Tell me what's wrong with his computer.

Mel: Well, the computer's broke.

Owl: Ummm, ok–big help–in what way is it broke?

Mel: I dunno–I tried everything.

Owl: (to original caller) Sir, would you please turn on your machine?

Caller: I can't.

Owl: Why not?

Caller: It's in pieces–Mel took it apart.

Mel: It said he had an error somewhere–I think the hard drive is shot, so I took it apart to look at it.

Owl: Ummm, well, what was the error?

Mel: Oh I dunno, something about the program something.

Caller: Mel said errors are bad.

Owl: Well, I don't know exactly what was wrong, but it seems you had a simple software error.

Mel: (to caller) Perhaps it was a simple software error.

Owl: Maybe you should run Scandisk.

Mel: (to caller) He's right, you should run Scandisk.

Owl: Call me back when the computer is back together sir, and we'll run Scandisk. Maybe we'll format your hard drive to reinstall things fresh.

Mel: (to caller) Starting fresh might fix it.

Caller: Ok, send a tech out to get this thing up and running again.

Owl: Ummm, no sir, my company won't do that–Mel is gonna hafta come over to put this back together again.

Caller: Oh…Mel…Mel? You there, Mel? Mellllllllllllllllllll…

She needs to be saved

Caller: Everytime I walk away from the computer, colored lines go on the screen.

Me: Does this happen all the time?

Caller: Yes, everytime I walk away.

Me: Do you have to reboot?

Caller: No, it goes away when I move the mouse.

Me: That sounds like your screensaver. Do you know what a screensaver is?

Caller: Isn't that when I save, it saves the screen? On disks?

yes, this really happened

I got this one too…

Caller: I set the screensaver for ten minutes, but it doesn't save anything.

I didn't really know what to say.…

He's ummmm…dumb?

Caller: (very mad) My damn printer hasn't worked in a month–fix it!

Me: Ok, ok. Calm down. Is it on now?

Caller: NO! I told you–it don't work.

Me: So there's no power to it?

Caller: That's what I said dammit–it don't work!

Me: Is it plugged in?

Caller: What do you think I am, stupid? It's plugged right there into the tower.

Me: Ummm, is it plugged into the wall?

Caller: The wall?

Me: You know—POWER.

Caller: Power…ummm…into the wall…lemme see…oh shit…*click*

Night Owl *(yes, it happened)*

Jason needed to refer the guy to Compaq to get a new driver. The caller wants to know if he should give them OUR contract number.

Jason: No, we are two different companies. They won't know us from Adam

Caller: "Huh…who's Adam?"

and it went downhill from there

The Phone-Line lady

Caller: I was on the phone with 'AOL' for three hours–they said my modem has no dialtone.

Me: Is the phone cord plugged in?

Caller: There's a phone cord?

Me: Yes, you need to plug the phone line to the back of the computer.

Caller: Ohhh–ok, I'll do that. I'll call you back if it doesn't work.…

Now, that was easy, right??? Well I didn't hear back from her until the following evening…

Caller: Remember me? The phone line lady? It didn't work. I get no dialtone.

Me: Hmmmm–well, before I get into the settings, could you double-check that cord?

Caller: Yes, one end is plugged into the computer, the other end I taped to the wall.

Me: Excuse me? You said you taped the other end to the wall? It's not hooked into a phone jack?

Caller: No, there's no phone hole in this room, so I taped it.

Me: Ummm, you need to hook that end up to a proper phone jack to get this to work.

Caller: But this is where I want the computer. I did what you said last night. It should work, right?

At this point I went into a detailed instruction on simple phone mechanics, wanting to slit my wrists the entire time.

Talk about feeling like a God

Caller: Hi–I'm stuck on playing my new game.

Me: What part are you stuck on?

Caller: It says click here to install. What should I do?

Me: Do you want to install it?

Caller: Yes.

Me: Then click where it says to.

Caller: Here?

Me: Yes–click here.

Caller: WOW! It's installing–how did you do that?

Me: Ummm…I just know these things.

Caller: Oh wait–now it says click OK to finish. Should I click OK?

Me: Yes.

Caller: Oh wow–it's finished–now it says click here to play. Should I click where it says?

Me: Yes.

Caller: WOW!! The games on…I never could have done this without you! I wish I knew as much as you…Thank you so much!

Whatever gave me that idea?

Caller: What size modem do I have?

Me: I don't know–what do your specs say?

Caller: Well, it says Pentium on it?

Me: That's your computer.
Caller: Whatever…well, I need more modems.
Me: What?
Caller: I should buy more modems…you know…upgrade…
Me: I think you mean MEMORY.
Caller: Whatever…should I buy more?
Me: I don't know. How much do you have?
Caller: I don't know. I think I'll buy more, though.
Me: I don't think you should do this. You should bring it to a shop.
Caller: Why?
Me: I don't think you should be opening the computer.
Caller: Whatever gave you that idea? I'm not stupid about these…

you be the judge…

Square peg in the round hole

Caller: There is no power to my new printer.
Me: Is it plugged in?
Caller: No.
Me: Well, that's why. Electricity travels through the power cord.
Caller: But the plug won't fit in the wall. The end is way too big. I tried to force it in, but it just won't fit.
Me: Ummm, I think I see your problem here. That cord is your printer cable–it goes to the computer.
The other cord, the AC plug–THAT one goes in the wall.
Caller: Well, why didn't they tell me this when I bought it?
Me: Well, it's clearly spelled out in the owner's manual.
Caller: Oh, I don't read those. Heh heh, they're not written for dumb people like me, you know…
Me: Apparently not**

** *These phrases were really uttered. Hers was sort of a "self abuse" statement said in jest. Mine was not–fully agreed with her statement at face value.*

He really needs to re-do the third grade

Caller: I hooked up my computer, but I have one cable left over.
Me: Well, do you see anything not hooked up?
Caller: I don't know–how do I tell?
Me: Look at it.
Caller: Oh, ok–what am I looking for?
Me: Ummm, something that's not hooked up.
Caller: Well, I don't see where the printer is hooked up.
Me: Does the cable fit the printer?
Caller: Yes.
Me: Well, I think we found the problem.
Caller: We did?
Me: Yes–hook the cable to your printer.
Caller: You sure–how do you know?
Me: Process of elimination.
Caller: What? Eminshon? No, I have an Epson.
Me: Listen, just hook the printer up.
Caller: Ok–wow, looks like I'm being good to go to town.*
Me: Ok sir—bye.

* He really said this

If people could only hear how dumb they sound when they talk to me. I'm
talking to a guy who needs to reinstall his printer.

Me: Start–Settings—Printers.
Caller: Start–Settings–Control Panel. I don't see Printers.
Me: Umm–I said Start–Settings–Printers. The words "Control Panel"
           never left my mouth.
Caller: Sorry–I'm in Printers. What now?
Me: Click once on your Printers icon so it's highlighted.
Caller: (click click)–OK, it's open.

Me: You clicked twice. I asked you to click once. Close it and start again.
Caller: Ok–I clicked once. It's highlighted.
Me: Good–press the delete key on the keyboard.
Caller: Delete? Where is that?
Me: Ummm, on the keyboard. It says either "delete" or "del".
Caller: I don't see it.
Me: Look harder.
Caller: Ohhhhh–there it is. Press it?
Me: (no–look at it idiot) Yes, press it.
Caller: It says "are you sure". Am I sure?
Me: Yes, you're sure....
Caller: You're sure about that?
Me: Just click yes.
Caller: Ok–Oh No–I'm defaulted. What did you do?
Me: No–it's just saying the new printer is XXXX.
Caller: Oh ok, got scared. What now?
Me: Get out the floppy disks for your printer.
Caller: Huh? Where are they?
Me: Ummm, I dunno–try the bottom right hand drawer of your desk?
Caller: I don't have a right hand drawer.

This one borders on the unbelievable, but it's 100% true. It didn't happen to me,–it happened to my fellow late night tech, Jason.

Caller: I installed a bunch of CD's, but the programs are missing.
Jason: Was the CD-ROM drive working?
Caller: Yes, I installed the CD's.
Jason: Well, let me install one with you to make sure you're doing it right. Open your CD drive.
Caller: My what?
Jason: Your CD-ROM drive–push the button.
Caller: I don't know what you mean.

Jason: Well, how did you install the CD's?
Caller: I just pushed them in the slot.
Jason: And where are they now?
Caller: I don't know—in the machine I guess.
Jason: Ummm, will you please gently tilt your tower?
Caller: *tilts tower—sound of falling CD's*

Ok, you get the point—the caller was shoving her CD's in one of the little cracks between the front panels on her computer, and they just fell inside. She thought she was "installing" them. When the computer was opened, there were over 20 CD's inside.

The scary part is, she actually EARNED enough money to buy a computer. Somebody PAYS her for something. Disturbing.

Callers never know what to call the computer—in actuality, they call it everything but. In this call, I use this to my advantage....

Me: "Ok, now turn off the computer."
Caller: "OK, the screens off."
Me: "Ummm—did you turn off the computer, though?"
Caller: "I turned off the screen—isn't that it?"
Me: "You need to turn off the computer, too."
Caller: "But there's nothing on the screen."
Me: "I KNOW—but did you turn off the COMPUTER—yes or no?"
Caller: "I don't know what you mean—the screen is off."
Me: (thinking "Ok, I'll play this game") "Ummm—turn off the modem, too"
Caller: "Ohhhh—the hard drive tower—why didn't you say so? Which button?"

Sometimes you just wanna scream

Let's pay with the MUTE button a bit. For those that don't know—we have a mute button that allows us to hear you, but you cannot hear us—We use it to say the things that would get us fired without you hearing us–we do this a lot, as this call will demonstrate. Muted words are in Italics.

Caller: My computer is slow.
Me: When did this start?
Caller: Right after I installed 'Microsoft Office'.
Me: How much RAM do you have?
Caller: I don't know.
Me: *Of course not, why would you know a silly thing like that??* Let's check (only 8mb). You'll need more RAM.
Caller: I need more RAM?
Me: *Did I stutter?* Yes–you need to upgrade.
Caller: But the clerk said this computer would work.
Me: *Three years ago, maybe.* Yes, but that program is using too much of your memory–you'll need more. *Please don't try to do this yourself.*
Caller: I can do this myself, right?
Me: *Heh heh–Grog smart–Grog open computer.* If you wish–are you sure you know how?
Caller: Well–it's easy, right? What do I need?
Me: *Grog confused–Grog use hammer.* Just the chips and a screwdriver.
Caller: Chips? I have to buy them?
Me: *Yes Grog…I mean Ebeneezer–break that wallet open.* Ummm–yes–you really should take this to a professional.
Caller: No–I'll go get me some "chips" now–I can do this.
Me: *Talk to you in an hour.* Ok sir–goodbye.

Ok, as I start to write this I've been at work for a bit more than an hour, and I've had 2 calls already today that I just had to share…

first one…

Caller: The planes are ruining my computer!
Me: Huh?

Caller: The planes! They're ruining my computer.

Me: Ok, Ok–tell me what happens.

Caller: When the planes fly, the computer freezes.

Me: (puzzled) Ok, when did this start happening?

Caller: Just yesterday.

Me: And how long have the planes been flying?

Caller: Since I've lived near the airport–6 years.

Me: Did you do anything different on the computer yesterday?

Caller: Well, I installed 'Microsoft Office'.

Me: (seeing by her history that the machine is 3 years old) How much RAM do you have?

Caller: I don't know (I check–8mb. Also has only 30mb hd left).

Me: Ummm, I don't think this has anything to do with the planes–you need to get a bit more RAM, and free up some hd space.

Caller: You mean spend money–oh no–it's the planes–send a guy out here.

Me: Ummmm, to do what? We're techs, not air traffic controllers.

Caller: I don't know–you're the tech–you guys figure it out. Just stop the planes from ruining my computer!

this went on and on and on...

I've been trying to help her retrieve her taskbar for the last 20 minutes

Me: "See the little gray line on the bottom of the screen?"

Her: "The gray one?"

Me: "Yes, the thin gray one."

Her: "All I see is a gray line."

Me: "I know–that's your taskbar–bring your mouse down to it."

Her: "I don't see the taskbar."

Me: (through gritted teeth) "Just–bring–the mouse–down–to–the–top –of–the—line."

Her: "The gray one?"

Me: "YES!!!!!!!!!!!!"

Her: "Ok, I did it–it's changed to an up arrow."
Me: "Good, now, click and hold the left mouse button"
Her: (clickclickclickclickclick) "Double click? Oops, I lost it."
Me: (about to slit my wrists) That's ok–just bring the mouse back down to the top of the line.
Her: "What line–the Gray one?"

arrrrrrrrrrrrggggggggggggggg!!!!!!!!!!!!!!!!!!

The mouse freezes–so does she

Caller: My mouse doesn't work.
Me: Tell me what happened.
Caller: I improperly shut down, now I'm at some Scandisk thing, and my mouse isn't there.
Me: Oh, that's no problem. The mouse won't show up in this screen. Just use your arrow keys to move the pointer and enter to select.
Caller: You mean the keyboard?
Me: (wondering what else I possibly could've meant) Yes.
Caller: How do I do that?
Me: See the keyboard–all you have to do is push the keys.
Caller: But there's so many–what do I do?
Me: See the four arrow keys–push the one pointing to the right.
Caller: Let's see…right…oops…no…oh, ok, got it–something on the screen moved. Did I do that?
Me: You sure did. See how it works? Use the arrows to move to an option, and then use enter to select it.
Caller: But how do I click on something?
Me: You use the enter key instead of clicking.
Caller: But I can't double click–this is too hard. I want my mouse back.
Me: Just press enter everytime the machine gives you a choice, ok? You'll end up in 'Windows'.

Caller: (finally listening to me) Look at that, I'm in 'Windows'…and my mouse is back. What do I do the next time the mouse goes away?

Me: For both of our sakes, let's pray that never happens…

Tell ya about the ABC's

Caller: I need a "D" drive and I don't have one.

Me: Huh?

Caller: The manual for my software says I need to type in "D:\setup" to install this–I don't have "D".

Me: (understanding the problem): Please read me the next line of the instructions.

Caller: It says "where 'D' is the letter of your CD-ROM drive".

Me: Get it? It's telling you to substitute your actual CD-ROM drive letter for "D". Just do that.

Caller: But my CD-ROM is "E".

Me: So type in "E" instead of "D".

Caller: But it asks for "D", not "E".

Me: FORGET "D"!!!!!!!! Just type in "E:\setup," OK?

Caller: Oh no–the instructions say "D", I need "D". I'm not messing up my computer.

Me: (wondering how someone could be SO dumb) Ok, let me see if I can explain this so you'll understand–remember algebra, in high school?

Caller: Yes.

Me: Where "X" really equaled something else…it's like that–most CD-ROM drives are "D", but some are not–they're telling you to substitute your letter, in this case, "E" for it. Understand?

Caller: "X"? I don't have a drive "X". You mean I need that also?

Now, when I talk to people, sometimes I just get frustrated. I usually don't hold back (but I won't abuse anyone), and I have said some things that make the other techs say "damn". Welcome to my world….

—Ma'am, you need to read the manual.

—Is there someone there who knows how to use this machine?

—Would you please tell the kids to shut up?

—You need to buy a better phone.

—Sir–can–someone–there–speak–better–English–than–you?

—Unregistered software, you know that's illegal, right?

—Teenage boys will find porn–yes, even your son.

—Well, somebody on your end downloaded that picture.

—Because it's a piece of junk, that's why...

—I'm here until midnight EST. Huh...what time is that in your time zone? What are you, kidding me?

—You really have no idea what you're doing, do you?

Fantasy Calls
or how some calls would go if I couldn't be fired

Crossing that Bridge

Callers always whine when the authorized service center is not RIGHT next door. This sorta happened.

Me: Well, it seems like your hard drive is shot. You'll need to take it to XYZ authorized service center in Anytown.

Caller: But that's too FAR awaaaaaaaaay.

Me: Ummm, I'm showing it's 10 miles. That's too far for you? Who are you, Boo Radley?

Caller: But I'll have to cross the bridge!

Me: Well, how far do you live from the bridge?

Caller: Right near it. I can see it from my house.

Me: Well listen up, Magellan. Did it ever occur to you that when you moved next to the bridge, that somehow, someday, you may have to leave your cave and CROSS it?

Caller: Isn't there something closer?

Me: (faking it) Well, lemme check…oh yea–right next door to you, there's "Mel's Computer and Bait Shop". Take it there. Mel seems about your speed.

Caller: Wow, next door to me. Must be a new place. I'll go there.

I HATE it when the phone isn't near the computer

Caller: I need help in 'Microsoft Word'.

Me: Ok, where are you now?

Caller: In the living room.

Me: No Einstein, where are you in the computer?

Caller: The computer? It's in the Den…Why?

Me: Oh no–don't tell me–the phone doesn't reach, right?

Caller: No, it doesn't. Is that a problem?

Me: Well, yea, it is. You're probably going to shout my instructions to Bettie Lou in the other room.

Caller: How did you know her name was Bettie Lou?

Me: It's a gift. Now, I'm assuming, impossible as this may seem, that Bettie Lou is dumber than you.

Caller: Well, kinda…we're simple people.

Me: Super-dumb and dumber. Listen, this is 1998–has the concept of a cordless phone somehow passed you by? Cause I'll tell ya, I refuse to work this way. I quit doing relay races in the seventh grade. Lemme ask you, did you make it to seventh grade?

Three strikes and you're out

Me: I'll need to know what kind of computer you have. What are the specs?

Caller: Ummmmm–I dunno–Pentium something?

Me: WRONG, IDIOT–try again.

Caller: Ummm–14" SVGA.

Me: That's the monitor, Stupid–one more chance.

Caller: (stuttering) Umm, uh (tries to find manual–landfill too far away) ummm (reads front of machine) Intel Inside!

Me: BZZZT–game over, Einstein–you failed the tech support test–we have found you too stupid to speak to us–thank you for calling.

I've always wanted to do this

Caller: (after a long tirade with me) "You're not very helpful–let me speak to your manager."

Me: "Certainly, hold on"…(deepens voice) "Manager speaking, can I help you?"

Caller: "Yes, your tech was very rude to me."

Me: "I'm sorry about that sir, but it's because you're an asshole."

Caller: "What?"

Me: "Yes, I heard the whole conversation. I'm surprised my tech didn't call you the dick you are."

Caller: "Are you saying I'm difficult?"

Me: "No, I'm saying you're a complete asshole. Please say you're sorry to the nice tech."

Caller: (meekly) "Okay…"

You don't meet the minimum

Caller: My new software won't work.

Me: What happened when you tried to install it?

Caller: I hit the disagree button on the license agreement–I don't have a software license.

Me: I'm sorry sir, you don't meet the minimum requirements for this software.

Caller: You mean my computer isn't big enough?

Me: No sir, your intelligence is too low. I'm sorry, but a minimum of 4 brain cells are needed to run this program. Thank you for calling.

I hate it when people cannot find something right in front of them

Me: Ok, now open Control Panel, and double click on the "Sounds" icon.

Caller: Sounds? I don't see a "Sounds" icon. It's not *(whining)* theeeeere!

Me: Listen dipshit, it's right in front of you. Just read each icon and click on the one that says "Sounds". You can read, right?

Caller: Oh, there it is! Right before "System". It was alphabetical. Who would've thought of that?

Me: Just about anyone with a third grade education. Bye…

Techs really hate it when you don't read the manual

Caller: I need help installing my printer.

Me: What part are you stuck on?

Caller: Installing it. Duh!

Me: Well, did you try what the manual says?

Caller: No, I didn't read it. It's too complicated.

Me: Yea, lots of three-syllable words in there. Ok, let's start. I want you to type FORMAT c:.

Caller: Why do we have to format my hard drive? I don't think this is part of the installation process.

Me: Well, how would you know that, sir? This is how I do it.

Caller: Ummmm…wait, before we do this, I'd like to check to see what the manual says to do.

Me: If you insist. Bye.

How about this lady…

Caller: We downloaded a virus by accident.

Me: Do you have an anti-virus program?

Caller: No.

Me: Well, you'll have to buy one.

Caller: WHAT! I'm not spending any money. I want you to fix it. Aren't you a tech? Isn't this your job?

Me: Oh yea, I keep forgetting. Ok.... "Abracadabra–Virus be gone!" There, all fixed.
Caller: Thank you. Goodbye.

The guy with the "Itchy Clickin' Finger"

Me: Ok, click on printers. Great. Now click once on your printer's icon.
Caller: (*Click Click*) Double Click?
Me: No. Click ONCE. ONE TIME! Not TWICE! NOOOOOO! You did it, didn't you? YOU FOOOOL!!!
Now it's ruined. FOREVER! Listen, Schmuck, learn to count before you EVER call me again!
Understand?

Note–Sorry. I spent forty-eight minutes today walking "the fastest mouse in the west" through deleting and reinstalling his printer. It was hell.

Dealing with the mentally challenged...

Me: Insert the disk. Click on Run. Now type "A:\setup".
Caller: Colon? How do you spell that?
Me: No. The punctuation mark. Two dots. Elementary school, remember?
Caller: Oh yea...(type type) It doesn't work.
Me: Are you sure you used a colon and not a semi-colon?
Caller: Huh? Oh, yeeeaaah...Wow, I couldn't tell the difference.
Me: And your computer can, meaning it's smarter than you. I suggest you destroy it before it takes over. Can you say "HAL"?

More Mentally challenged...

Caller: My computer says there's not enough memory and it's slow.
Me: (check HDD space left). Your hard drive is completely full.
Caller: That means I can't put more programs on here, right?
Me: Your understanding of the completely obvious is amazing.
Caller: Huh?

Me: Never mind. Let's delete some programs (Delete...delete...).
Caller: Wow, now I have some space. I can fill it up again!
Me: I wouldn't fill it completely up again, sir.
Caller: But how can I keep that from happening? What causes this?
Me: It probably has something to do with that room temperature IQ.
Caller: Huh?
Me: Never mind sir—save away! Thank you for calling.

How did this guy EARN the money to buy a computer...

Caller: I need help saving to a disk.
Me: Wait a minute—I see here you've owned this computer for two years.
Caller: Yes.
Me: You've had it two years, and you STILL can't use a floppy?
Caller: It's just so confusing.
Me: For monkeys, maybe. Listen pal, there's no hope for you.
Caller: There's not? Oh no. That means...
Me: Yes—You need to slit your wrists before you cause further damage.
Caller: Can you walk me through that?
Me: Gladly.

If Evil Owl had his way, tech support hold messages would sound like this...

Thank you for calling technical support. All our technicians are either busy or in the middle of an important download. Since your problem is most likely trivial, we would appreciate you waiting until a tech feels like picking up the line, or hell freezes over, whichever comes first. Dress warm.

Thank you for calling Tech Support. If you are calling from a touch tone phone, chances are it's set to pulse, so asking you to push buttons is irrelevant. For your listening pleasure, here's Barry Manilow singing "Mandy" over and over and over....

Thank you for calling technical support. In order to make your call go smoothly, please do the following:

#1–Boot your computer.
#2–That means your computer must have power running through it.
#3–No–that's the monitor. The box under your desk...yes, the tower. Turn it on.
#4–See the screaming child next to you? Yes? Shoot him.
#5–Get out all floppies....
#6–They're in the bottom left hand drawer.
#7–We're watching you, that's how we knew that.

Thank you for calling tech support. We would like to express our complete surprise that you were able to correctly dial the phone. Of course, you probably messed that up and reached us by accident. Stay on the line anyway, we could use the laugh.

Thank you for calling technical support. All our techs are busy performing the nightly pagan sacrifice to the almighty coffee machine. Stay on the line, the first available tech will be with you shortly (music plays).... Your call is important to us, as we haven't laughed in a quite a bit, so please stay on the line, a tech will be with you shortly...(more music)...hey, you know what happened yesterday? Some loser called us with a simple little problem, and we WIPED HIS HARD DRIVE...hahahahahaha...*chuckle* stay on the line, we REALLY wanna talk to you...(even more music)...I'll have to ask you to stop pushing keys. See, we're in your hard drive now, looking at that downloads folder–WHOA!! Where did you find THAT one??...(still more music)...well, the day is done, and we've decided your call wasn't that important after all. Better luck tomorrow * click *

Night Owl Poetry

I love formatting hard drives. There is nothing quite like destroying months and months of some idiot's work. It never fails—the biggest idiots are the ones who never back up. It gives me great pleasure to listen to the tirade when I tell them there is nothing else I can do. All you techs out there know exactly what I mean. I like the format so much, I wrote a little poem:

Ode to a Format

Oh mighty Format,
I sing my praise of thee,
thy power, thy completeness,
so easy and hassle free.

Oh Mighty Format,
destroy thy data corrupt,
grind it into utter nothingness,
along with the stuff not backed up.

The user will cry and curse,
convulse in a mighty wail,
for now Quicken is lost for good,
along with the precious e-mail.

"I don't have the disks," they say,
"to load back the stuff you trashed,"
"I smile and tell the whiny pirate,"
"twas bootlegging the reason you crashed."

"I should have learned to back up,"
"but in the manual I refused to look,"
"An IQ of 60 is required," I say,
"so I doubt you could read the book."

I praise you mighty Format,
although they call me a conniver,
for wait until they find they cannot reinstall
without the CD ROM driver.

Sung to the tune of the Beatles "Let it Be"

ahem

When a user calls me with some trouble
And I feel that he's been rude to me
I speak my words of wisdom

Format C

In the user's hour of darkness
the solution's right in front of me
Owl's words of wisdom

Format C

Format C, Format C,
Format C, yea Format C
Theeeeere goes your data–Format C

And when the broken hearted user
gives me the "no backups" plea
I giggle when I tell him

Format C

Even though they may be angry
Still a chance that they will see
How much I enjoy saying it

Format C

Format C, Format C
Format C, Yea, Format C
Owl's words of wisdom–Format C

The user frets and he is grouchy
There's still a light that gives me glee,
Until he calls tomorrow,

Format C

I hang up to the sound of swearing
another user angry at me
Because he didn't back up

Format C

Format C, Format C
Format C, yea Format C

theeeeere goes your data
Format C.

Mel

Some of you callers have this one good friend,
who you claim knows computers "real well",
this friend is an "expert", you always say,
for sake of argument, let's call him Mel.

Mel has already tried to fix it, you see,
he says it's broke, no point in me trying,
When I hear this, I always hold a chuckle inside,
cause I know most of the time, Mel's lying.

Mel owns several floppy disks and uses big words,
has "DOS for Dummies"–you called him first,
Mel sat down and tried a few tricks he knew,
and proceeded to make your problem worse.

That file he zapped was an important one,
the computer needed it to run properly, you see,
I may not be able to undo his silly mistake,
oh well, at least you got it ruined for free.

Mel will always blame it on something else,
that's totally unrelated to the damage he's caused,
When I try to question Mel as to the problem's nature,
Mel stutters and stammers, his brain obviously paused.

You listen to Mel, you want to argue with me,
you don't listen to the advice I'm giving,
You have to realize I fix computers by trade,
while Mel sells cars for a living.

I don't mind working with a friend of yours,
but he should listen and put the ego to rest,
cause I'll find out soon what he really does know,
He's gonna have to pass The Owl Test.

He fails if the error message isn't written down,
he fails if the computer is off or it's apart,
If he tells me about his computer at home, he fails,
or if he has trouble with the button called "start".

When that happens, I can't take his word for it,
I fix them over the phone, it's how I earn my pay,
I've grown quite attached to that weekly check,
And I would really like to keep it that way.

So keep Mel calm, ask him to work *with* me,
if you don't, your computer might be a wreck,
the only time you can really trust your friend,
is if your friend happens to be a fellow tech.

A plea to the Mel Army

This is not to say that if you're *not* a tech, you can't help your friends—all I ask is that you work *with* me and let me do my job. If you really know computers, I'll know it.

TECH HELL

In 1980 my girlfriend took a college course on the BASIC programming language. I read the book one night and the next day I asked her instructor if that was all there was to it. He said yes. I asked him if they paid people to do this. He said yes. So I learned BASIC, then FORTRAN, then Pascal, then assembly language and so on.

Even though I grew up in a rural environment, I always had an aptitude for electronics. Take enough old radios and amplifiers apart and you figure out some stuff. I studied enough to know what the basic components are and their function. Computers seemed like a natural extension of TTL electronics.

So I prostituted myself doing computer related jobs to gain experience until someone would hire me as a programmer. Been doing it ever since. Once in a while I work in the hardware end of the business. My troubleshooting skills seem to be very useful and accurate. Mostly I program; Java right now, who knows what is next. I'm sure it will be interesting.

Around 1986 I read a story on the FIDO-NET. It was titled the "Bastard Admin from Hell". I immediately understood that this was a technical variation of a MAD Magazine storyline. I liked the idea and decided to create a list of Tech Support "what we really wanted to say" quotes. We fleshed out the concept while on an airplane flying from Santa Monica California to Phoenix Arizona (returning from a visit to the Getty Museum).

At the time there was no real outlet other than FIDO-NET, but the stories spread and I gathered more from contributors. When I worked for 'AOL' in the tech support department I learned HTML and set up the original TECH-HELL. It was based in the Netherlands on a UNIX server (Web searches for TECHHELL that return an address of http://130.89.233.61/~wena/tech-hell.html are referring to the original techhell. Old school!).

Tech Hell started out as a performance art piece that was supposed to feed itself by using some ASP scripts and an Access MDB file. It was a point of commiseration for the unappreciated. The place where "good techs go to cry". Soon it got large enough that it needed it's own home and I coughed up the dinero to buy www.techhell.com. Note that Yahoo still returns Techhell all alone. Art is something that elicits an immediate emotional response from the viewer. Look at all the web pages that reference Techhell, and what they say about it. I'd say that Techhell made us artists. We took the site down for six months and I got hundreds of emails asking what happened and I personally answered each one explaining that the site was no longer unique, the entries had become humorless vulgarities and that left us unfulfilled.

After a while we started a Cable Access show called "Tech X". We offered free computer technical support to anyone who would call in, but the rule was that we got to say what we really wanted to say when the caller was shown to be the root cause of the problem. If you have ever watched cable access shows you know that the audience is high spirited and we soon stopped offering support and instead played a Jeopardy style game and gave away t-shirts with seminude women on them. That seemed to attract a crowd. Saturday night at 10pm for almost two years. Sadly, new employment forced the breakup of our cast and crew and the Tech X show is nothing more than video taped memories.

Technical support customers? I liked them. They paid my rent, bought me food and supplied me with all of life's essential needs. In exchange I was to listen to them describe an issue, decipher what was really wrong and then instruct them how to resolve the issue.

I used to work in a slaughterhouse. I've worked in telephone boiler rooms, as a fruit picker, as a tractor driver, for crooked service station owners, as a baby-sitter for strippers, crewed on sail boats in Hawaii, pimped, acted as a personal bodyguard and as a collections agent.

Telephone technical support is easy compared to those jobs. No one ever takes swings at me or throws things at me or tries to shoot me. There is air-conditioning and a comfy chair. I can juggle, draw or do almost anything else I want while I take the call. I sit in front of a computer and play the guessing game. I take guesses at what you did to the computer, based on what you tell me, and if I guess right I get a short call and you go away happy. I had very short call times. I guess really well. After 100,000 calls it becomes second nature.

All in all I found that if you told the truth, laid out what you were going to do BEFORE you started and made sure the customer understood the possible outcomes and their statistical likelihood, it went pretty smooth.

Remember what we demand! We have your name!

Email: RipTayness@techhell.com
Website: http://www.techhell.com.

Editor's note: I ran into an interesting message board on Techhell, where call center technicians can post "do's and don'ts" for customers. Hatred seems to be a very common theme. I've listed 25 rants for each section. Enjoy!

25 Do's

DO attempt to comprehend what you are agreeing to and when it says you will need a credit card to register; understand that this means you need a credit card to sign up for our service, YOU SLACKJAWED HILLBILLY!

DO be honest and tell me the truth about what you deleted.

DO be prepared to be put on hold for a long time, especially if you're an arsehole.

DO complain about how it's "negligent" for Company A's software to be interfering with Company B's. It's called "Windows"–deal with it.

DO ask for my supervisor so that he can give you an even dumber explanation for our apparent inability to deal with your ignorance…

DO realize that we have much more experience of pissing customers off than they have of pissing us off.

DO remember you called ME. So when you tell me that I don't know anything, you will then recall the fact that you are asking me—not the other way around.

DO get out of the tub with your nice new expensive laptop so you can reset your modem!

DO get yourself a newer computer, not the P90 that you son-in-law gave to you because he bought a new one.

DO go to the bathroom before you call.

DO have a 10-year-old child present so I can talk to someone who knows what to do.

DO have the balls to follow through on your threat to close your account with us.

DO insist on complaining to a supervisor, so he can take your verbal abuse and then transfer you back to me to try and fix your dumb problem.

DO lie down on a busy highway.

DO learn the language of the country you reside in…or play queue roulette!

DO piss off your tech, so we can double bill you, erase your account, change your password so many times, and we have access to every virus and macro to send to you…hehehe…

DO plug a toaster in, throw it in the tub, and take a bath.

DO realize you are calling for tech support, not a personal counselor.

DO remove your head from your rectum before calling me.

DO restart your computer at least once a year. No, it does not shorten the life span of your computer, but your life span will be much shorter if you tell me that again.

DO tell me how you are losing $7000 dollars a day because your $50 a month consumer level DSL is down. Hmmm, ya think maybe you could afford the Business class service?

DO thank your lucky stars that I can't reach through the phone and choke your dumb ass.

DO write some of this shit down so that we don't have to put up with your bullshit when you call us ten more times on the same day!

DO a favor to every tech agent…. DON'T REPRODUCE…because obviously your family breeds MENTALLY CHALLENGED SHAVED MONKEYS.

25 Don'ts

DON'T act like you know more than you do. We know that you know nothing.

DON'T ask for a manager. They don't even know how to use their own computer.

DON'T ask me if I have a direct line, because even if I did, do you really think I would give it to you?

DON'T ask the tech "Can you see what's on my screen?" No, dumbass, we can't magically transform your phone into a viewing screen any more than you can use your computer without screwing it up.

DON'T attempt to threaten legal action on us, as you will be paying for our lawyers as well as your own. So if you don't go broke first, you will undoubtedly lose the case and be forced to pay US money. Now, if you read the agreement you would have seen this and never even considered such a moronic statement.

DON'T brag to us about your MCSE++, your position as a Network Admin, or your copious quantity of personal knowledge. If you're THAT good, fix it yourself.

DON'T bring your friends, family, church and neighbors along for moral support.

DON'T call on behalf of your son or daughter who attends one of our fine institutions of higher learning. S/he may not know what the hell is wrong with the gerbil-powered system you bought for college, but you sure as shit don't know what the error messages say. Don't even *try* it.

DON'T call unless you have eliminated all possibilities listed in your manual, given to you by the geek kid down the street, and called Dial-a-Prayer a few times to exorcise the demons from your system.

DON'T tell me your life story unless you are cute, single and have pictures!

DON'T ask me to credit your account, because even if I could, I wouldn't give you shit.

DON'T assume that a tech knows everything. A tech is just a person—they make errors, too. You may have misled them or they may not know the information that is required. A tech is not a computer literate person by definition, just someone looking for free ISP support or low earning in a usually comfy chair.

DON'T assume that threatening us will make us even remotely care about your issue any more then I do now, which is about how much I care about that piece of lint that is stuck up your ass.

DON'T brag to me that someone is paying you $25.00/hour to set up their computer when I'm getting paid $8.00/hour to talk YOU through it.

DON'T get nasty and explain that "you don't have time to learn to do it. Just fix it"–we go from helpful to "oops, that looked important" in well under 5 seconds.

DON'T tell me your name is "Dr. So-and-so" Or else you can call me Technician Sir for the rest of the call!

DON'T expect me to care. It's just a job.

DON'T insult the Tech you are talking to while they are editing your SYSTEM.INI file or working in your SYSTEM folder.

DON'T say 'this computer has never worked' and then tell us about the 50 million programs that you somehow miraculously installed.

DON'T spend twenty minutes talking about how much you enjoy your new computer. I have a PII 400 at home. If you make me jealous enough I just might say: "Ok, Exit to DOS...Now type: f-o-r-m-a-t..."

DON'T start off the call by telling us how many times you have called. We really don't care. It's not like you are going to get a prize for being the first person to call tech support 20 times.

DON'T start your call with yelling at the tech. You wouldn't call your "Brain Surgeon" an "Asshole" and ask if he was sure of what he was doing before a lobotomy.

DON'T tell me you don't believe in electromagnetic interference. I suppose you don't believe in AIDS either. Good, go test that theory, please.

DON'T think I am God—I humbly admit I am not. If I was and I created you in my image, you would not be such a technical failure.

DON'T think independently...we don't encourage it at all.

Um, thanks. I think

This was just a standard call, cooperative customer (one of the few I've ever had) and as soon as I've got the guy's 'Outlook Express' configured, I ask him if there's anything else I can do for him (crossing my fingers that there isn't). 'No, that's all, you've been delicious' and then hangs up. Were he and I having the same conversation?

Sub has cross-dressing issues...

Lady called me, said she occasionally monitors her 13-year-old son's e-mail account.... Today she found a number of e-mails being sent every other day of a man whose face was concealed, and he was dressed as a woman...Every successive mail-out the individual has less clothing on...The lady wanted to know if anyone could have hacked into her sons account and been routing these disturbing e-mails through it. I explained to her that it was possible, but very unlikely, a good virus scanner may be able to find a virus that allows someone to do this...(Trojan...) The lady paused for a few seconds.

Next thing I heard was "Oh God—The furniture—it's mine!!! These pictures were taken in MY HOUSE!!!! Click—

Space Station...

Tech: Can I have you type n-e-t space u-s-e?
User: That didn't work.
Tech: What did it say?
User: The name specified is not recognized as an internal or external command, operable program or batch file.
Tech: What exactly did you type?
User: n-e-t-s-p-a-c-e-u-s-e
Tech: This time instead of space, type in n-e-t, press the spacebar and then type in u-s-e.
User: Oh, duh, I feel so stupid. You're not going to submit this to one of those stupid user things, are you?
Tech: No, I wouldn't do that.

Slow Joe....

Salesmen Samples...

Customer: "I've got a modem and it came with your software. The salesman said this is all I need. How do I set it up?"
Tech: "Put the disk in the drive".
Customer: "What drive?"
Tech: "Do you have a computer?"
Customer: "No."
Tech: "Go ask the salesman how. Obviously he knows something the rest of the world doesn't."

Printer

A customer called me asking where he could download a printer on the internet. I explained that this might not be possible until we overcome the translation of bits to atoms.

Pet peeves of mine…

Some things that customers do or say that *really* get to me some days…

*Calling ink cartridges 'cartilidges' Duh!
*Putting ME on hold…goodbye. Actually some days, this is kinda nice, but it ruins your call times…
*In response to "Do you have the serial number for that printer?" they answer with a simple "No"…that's it, just "No." Well, could you go get it for me, hmmm?"
*The "I just have a quick question…" type. Yeah, sure ya do…20 minutes and 20 questions later, still on the line…quick question indeed.
*The argumentative type. "I don't think that is the problem" or "I doubt that will fix it". Then WHY the heck did you call me? This is not Monty Python and I am not a professional arguer, ok?

Password Nightmare

I work for a free ISP in the UK. One of the calls I got recently was as follows…

Customer:	I can't log on.
Me:	Ok. Could be a number of reasons. What password are you using?
Customer:	Well, not the one you gave me, that's for sure.
Me:	Ah…you've not been using our password…why?
Customer:	Every time I type that in it comes up as a load of little stars.
Me:	Yeah, so what password have you been using?
Customer:	*********
Me:	Your password is encrypted and that's why it comes up as stars.

Customer: So, my password is encrypted.
     Me: Yeah.
Customer: So, how do you spell that?

At this point I 'accidentally' pressed the release key

Nice Jargon

I work tech support for a government agency and our users are not exactly up on the techie jargon. Some examples:

"Yeah, my laptop is not turning on properly. I think you should replace my motherlode."
"Look, I have been programming in WWW and I know a thing or two…"
"My boyfriend knows computers and he says I need more BAM if I am to work any faster!"
"When are we going to get Microsoft Expel?"

Network Nitwit

I had a customer call (an Indian customer, no less) and begin to yell at me because he could not find the RJ 45 jack in which to connect his cable modem. The customer stated that he just purchased the NIC and could not find the jack. After 20 minutes of describing what the jack looked like and listening to this guy impugn my technical abilities in 2 different languages, I finally asked the cust which PCI slot he installed the card into. He said, "Nowhere, it is sitting on the table next to the computer". The call ended with the customer apologizing alot and me laughing.

need the SYSTEM with you

I work as a CD writer tech. I received a call from a user that was having problems with his writer locking up while starting the process to burn an audio Cd. I asked him to click on the writer icon and walk me through the process he takes. He stated he was not at his computer. I then explained the need for him to be at his computer. He became VERY upset, stating that when he called a few hours earlier, the person only told him he had to be with his CD burner. He had gone home at lunch and brought the CD writer to work with him. There was no computer available at his work either.

Nabib....

Tech A: Thank you for calling <deleted Major computer companyname>, how may I help you?
Mr. J.D.: I am not seeming to be connecting.
Tech A: Ok, what kind of error message to you get?
Mr. J.D.: I do not know, just help me!

This is common, we have people who will tell us they saw the error message 10+ times but have absolutely no idea what it said. We are not psychics; we must know what it said to know what the problem is.

Tech A: Oh, ok, well, what kind of computer do you have?
Mr. J.D.: It is being a Packard Bell.
Tech A: Do you know how much memory you have?
Mr. J.D.: I have 4 megs of Random Memory.

Here is our problem, less than the minimum requirements. Now you would think that once the person finds out they don't have the right equipment to run our software, that would be the end of the conversation. But the following dialogue is the most common response...

Tech A: I'm sorry, but, you don't meet the minimum requirements, so, we're really not of much use to you until you upgrade.
Mr. J.D.: (quite agitated) But, this is not explaining why I am not connecting! Why am I not connecting to your system!? What does memory have to do with me connecting?!

Tech A: Well, if you don't meet the requirements, there is no guarantee that the software will work at all, hence the system requirements. Because you don't meet them, there's really no reason to try and fix it, because it's not going to work.

Mr. J.D.: BUT, I HAVE A 28.8?! What would you have done if I had said I had 8 Megs?!

We commonly have people call in and find out they do not meet the minimum requirements. They will then call back and tell the next person they talk to that they HAVE the proper amount. What they don't realize is we keep a database on all calls. The last tech you spoke to noted that you only had...

Tech A: Well, when I found that you had four, after you told me that you surely had eight, I would be pretty mad.

Mr. J.D.: This is not explaining why I am not connecting! I HAVE A 28.8! Changing the subject will not work.

Tech A: But you do NOT have the MEMORY requirements for the software. It WILL NOT work for you unless you upgrade to eight megs of RAM.

Mr. J.D.: I am thinking that I must be canceling my account...

We hate to lose your business, but we also require that you help us. We are always amazed that people don't want to believe that there are minimum requirements to using a piece of software. Especially because its printed all over the package.

Monkey Man

Being one of those rare females in the tech support business, I deal with a lot of different things–from, "You'd make a great phone sex operator" to "You don't know what you're talking about, you're just a girl." Nothing will beat the time I was on the phone with this older gentleman for about 40 minutes, trying to get his (of all things) caller id box working properly.

Towards the end of the call, I had the guy on speakerphone so that my cubemates could hear what I had to go through with him. Suddenly, he stated, "You're more fun to talk to then playing with my monkey." I didn't know what to say to that, so I replied back with a straight face, "I would-n't know sir, I've never played with a monkey." He said that that was too bad. About half a minute later, another girl, who sat 3 cubes away and did-n't know I was on the phone, walked into the cube with her hands over her head, acting like a monkey. I started laughing so hard that I couldn't breathe and I didn't have time to mute the phone. Suddenly, the customer stated, "You know what causes heavy breathing don't you?" I hung up on him immediately after that.

Looking for a job

I worked in a company's in-house tech center. This lady called in asking if the internet was down. I proceeded to check mine and said, "Mine works, what seems to be the problem," she replied: "I'm trying to access this web-site and it keeps saying error." I asked for the web address and went to the website and it looked just fine. Then she told me to click on the Careers section and try to submit for a job, sure enough an error. I told her that I couldn't help her with an outside website if her internet was working. She replied: "Well how the hell can I get a job outside of this company if you people won't help me?!"

inka, stinka....

Tech Q: Thank you for calling <name of company>! May I have your name and phone number please?

Average Joe: My name is Average Joe. My phone number is <some number>.

Tech Q: How may I help you Joe?

Average Joe: I happened to try another product that is not made by your company. The damn thing has leaked all over my printer!

Tech Q: Well, you know that this is not covered over our warranty. If you want it to be serviced or repaired you are going to have to pay for this.

Average Joe: I didn't know that and I didn't know this would happen! Your warranty says you cover ink spilling into the printer.

At this point I would like to say to the customer to RTFM (Read the ummmmm yes Fine…Fine Manual)

Tech Q: Sir, on page <manual page> it says, "do not try to refill or use another type of cartridge that is not made by <company name>".

Average Joe: I did not know this! So you're damn well saying I have to pay to get the printer fixed?

Tech Q: Yes, Joe.

Average Joe: Well, that is really great!

At this point I am thinking to myself. Well if you RTFM then you would have known. But NOOOOOooooooooo! You had to be a Smart Arse and call us to tell you of your trouble.

Tech Q: <A second of where the mute button is on laughing your head off>. Well Joe I am truly sorry for the inconvenience. <think you're such a smuck>

Average Joe: Well, I want to talk to a supervisor! Right now!

Tech Q: Sorry sir, but my supervisor is going to tell you the same thing.

Average Joe: I think your company is f*cking crap! I am going to get my lawyer to sue your company.

Tech Q: <go ahead, it is in our manual, which you should have read before doing this> Well, Sir, you can do that.

Average Joe: Well, I am going to do this right now! Good F*cking bye! <Click as the phone hangs up.>

Well we now think you are a pompous ass, but if you want to tell the whole world, be our guest.

I LOVE YOU VIRUS

I am a tech support lead and we were very busy receiving calls from people that had infected their systems with the ILOVEYOU virus…I received this amusing call:

Tech: Thank you for calling—technical support, how may I help you?
Customer: Yes, I got that ILOVEYOU thing in my email and I opened it
Tech: Ok, sir, don't worry. It's happening everywhere…did you reboot your machine after opening it?
Customer: No.
Tech: Good…I am gonna walk you through deleting some vbs files and then we will run a Norton or McAfee fix…ok?
Customer: You know…I never get e-mail…ever…and my eyes lit up when I got a message that said somebody loves me…I mean I was so happy…then this shit happens…what a kick in the head.
Tech: Yes Sir, Love Stinks.

Forest for the trees

A lady called up stating that the keyboard to her 'Mac' wasn't working and asked which port she should be putting the plug into. I replied that either one should work, to which the lady said: "Well there's one that works and one that doesn't. Which one should I use?" Me: *three second pause* "Use the one that works." Lady: "OHHHHH, thanks." Suffice it to say that this one took the cake for call of the week at the office.

Failure to Communicate

After explaining at length to a customer that their password was case sensitive, they sent an email stating the following: "I was told by one of your people that my password was 'k' sensitive. I have tried typing my password with the 'k's and without the 'k's and neither has worked. Please tell me what I am doing wrong."

Don't call me

This advice is based upon 3 years of funny and unfunny experiences as a tech. If you can't reboot your computer, don't call me. If you don't know where the start button is, don't call me. If you have some kind of moral objection to loading the newest version of our software, don't call me. If you don't meet the system resources to run our software, don't call me. If you want to have an involved debate about the CEO of my company and his politics, I don't care; the man pays my bills. Don't call me. If your dog is on fire, and you are convinced it's because of the aliens that program our software, call Jerry Springer, call Sally, call Oprah, but don't call me. If you are in labor, don't call me. I don't care if you think I sound like the recording. I don't care to be called princess, darling, love, sweetie, honey, kitten, or missy. I also don't care if you intend to sue my company, just leave me out of it. Most of all…if you aren't going to listen to me and let me help you, don't call me.

Did I or did I not say…

Ok if this story doesn't may you want to quit your wonderful and rewarding job of tech support I don't know what will:

Me: Thank you for calling____My name is ____how may I help you?
Cust: My cable light is flashing.
Me: Well then we're going to have to transfer you to our cable modem department, but unfortunately they're office is closed on Sundays.
Cust: What!!! You're supposed to be 24 hours!
Me: Yes Tech Support is open 24-7. I am tech support, but that office isn't open on Sundays.
Cust: Well I haven't had service in 3 hours and I want a credit for not being on!
Me: Sir the office that handles credits is closed on Sundays.
Cust: Well then I want to cancel my service!

Me:	Sir the office that handles your flashing cable, is the same office that handles you being granted a credit, and oh yes, that very same office can cancel your service, BUT THEIR OFFICE IS C-L-O-S-E-D ON SUNDAYS!
Cust:	So they're closed today?
Me:	Is today Sunday?
Cust:	Yes.
Me:	Then they're closed.

Anti virus man

I do tech support for a major computer company and on a boring night I got this call…

Caller:	Yeah, I think I have a virus.
Me:	And why do you think that?
Caller:	'Cuz it's slow.
Me:	Um, what is?
Caller:	My action is.
Me:	Your action? What action?
Caller:	My computer has a virus.
Me:	What antivirus do you have?
Caller:	I have McAfee but I never use it…
Me:	Well, why don't you use it? (laughing hysterically)
Caller:	It slows everything down.
Me:	Well, isn't your action slow now?
Caller:	Yeah, that McAfee slowed me down.
Me:	How do you know it's a virus if you never use McAfee?
Caller:	Look man, some things in life you just know and I know this.
Me:	And how do you know this?
Caller:	I can't take this anymore.
Me:	Huh? (loud crash in background)

Caller: There, the damn computer is dead. Are you happy now?

   Me: (actually fell out of my chair from laughter) Uh, yes I am, thank you, have a good night.

7-10 bucks an hour

I was taking a supervisor call and the customer became very upset with me. I wouldn't walk him though setting up his e-mail because he was using 'Microsoft Outlook', which we do not support. His response was: "Well you know the real difference between you and me? I make about 30 times your 7-10 dollar hourly wage." I responded: "You want to know another big difference Sir? I can get my e-mail." *Click*

QUOTES:

"I feel so much better now......just like taking a big poop...."
The other day one of my coworkers helped a woman with a very lengthy problem (one which the woman's husband forbade her to call us for help on). After being helped, the woman responded with this quote.

"Does this software no longer work because of what Janet Reno said?"
This was from a customer whose Internet Explorer told them that it had performed an illegal operation.

"It says I've performed an Illegal Operation and will be shut down. Have I done something wrong?"
Sometimes I feel like saying "Yes and we are reporting you to the authorities now." or "RUN! RUN!" or "And just what were you doing?"

"A White One."
This is the answer I got when I asked her "What type of computer do you have"

"But I'm Left handed…"
This is the response I got when I said "please right click on the icon."

"OH GOD, I was afraid you were gonna ask that. The whole time I was on hold the recording said I'd need it, but I didn't think you'd need it for this...."
Inconceivable response to, "May I have your Serial Number please"?

"Do I have to be online to download a file?"
"Sir, Do you have to plug in your TV before you watch it?" What are we? Magicians? Hey, if I could download files without being online I would NEVER pay for an online service again.

"I tried and I tried, But it just won't fit...."
This is what the caller said about our install disks. He got through the first one, but he was stumped when it asked him to insert the second disk. It never occurred to him to remove Disk #1 BEFORE trying to insert Disk #2.

"a stuffed animal that my boyfriend got me at the grocery store"
This is the usual response to *"What's on your screen right now?"* The proper response to their answer is *"For god sakes!! Get that off of there!!!!"*

"It just comes up with a message and says click OK...now what?"
When it's late and the caller gives me this line for the sixty-third time in one call. I've been known to dream of high-powered rifles and clips full of ammo. A dark night. A large tree to climb. A well lit trail to watch over.

"Is the internet down?"
Yes. The internet went down about 5 minutes ago when I went out for a cigarette and tripped on the cord that plugged the internet in...just give me 3 minutes and I'll have it right back up. Sheesh.

"Is that the letter zero or the number zero?"
This happens when we are dictating a configuration to a caller. What universe do these people come from that has a LETTER zero? I like to ask *"...and what letter comes before zero please?"* The other variation on this is *"Is that a lower case or upper case zero?"*

"Is this a LIVE person?"
Well depending on what time of the day you call and how many stupid people I converse with today. Actually I always find this response amusing. It goes along with the caller who pushes the buttons on his touch tone phone when we ask for the telephone number and area code. Those sillies.

RINKWORKS

My experience in the computer industry is as a software engineer. I've been a software engineer for seven years now. I've never worked in technical support, where most stories of such clueless computer users come from, but I often mind myself in informal situations where users consult my opinion. This was more the case in school than recently, where users would, for some reason, gravitate toward me when I worked in my university's computer clusters to ask questions.

I started RinkWorks in 1997. At-A-Glance Film Reviews existed before that, in mid-1996. When Book-A-Minute came along, the RinkWorks name was created to bind the two features under a common brand name. Computer Stupidities debuted on RinkWorks a month after RinkWorks itself did, in January 1998.

What do I think of customers? Nothing much, as a collective group. We're all customers. Consumers of computer software keep me employed. Were I a technical support representative, I'd consider *clueless* computer users my job security. Despite the seeming mass-scale mockery of computer consumers on my web page, I think all of us have mental lapses at times. The ridicule on Computer Stupidities is meant to be good-natured, for the most part. If I'm inclined to be truly derisive, it's not so much at the stupidity but the belligerence exhibited in some of the anecdotes: stories of people who are not just unknowing but in denial about it. Some people are too proud to admit when something is their own fault or their own ignorance, so they get angry and defensive and blame everybody but themselves, particularly the technical support representatives who are trying to help. I can't respect that. But all of us have a synapse misfire now and then, and there's no dishonor in lacking omniscience or perfection.

—Samuel Stoddard

Editor's Note: *Computer Stupidities* surpassed 1000 anecdotes on April 9, 1999. You can find tons of laughs there. The site cannot accept new anecdote submissions as it is backlogged by nearly 800 submissions. Check out this website at: http://www.rinkworks.com/stupid.

- **Tech Support:** "Type 'fix' with an 'f'."
- **Customer:** "Is that 'f' as in 'fix'?"

- **Tech Support:** "Tell me, is the cursor still there?"
- **Customer:** "No, I'm alone right now."

- **Tech Support:** "Do you have 3 1/2 inch diskettes?"
- **Customer:** "No, I only have 3 of them."

I was showing a new user how to change her password. She was typing the new one in slowly and said to me, "I hope you're not reading my password." I replied that I was the system administrator and didn't need her password. She replied, "That's good to know. I wouldn't want you accessing my stuff."

Me: "You type 'win' to start up Windows 95."
A Friend: *(in awe)* "How come you know all those commands by heart? Did you get a list of them somewhere?"

Tech Support: "Just call us back if there's a problem. We're open 24 hours."
Customer: "Is that Eastern time?"

I had this conversation recently with a lady who swore she had been using computers since forever.

- **Tech Support:** "All right. Now click 'OK'."
- **Customer:** "Click 'OK'?"
- **Tech Support:** "Yes, click 'OK'."
- **Customer:** "Click 'OK'?"
- **Tech Support:** "That's right. Click 'OK'."
- **Customer:** "So I click 'OK', right?"
- **Tech Support:** "Right. Click 'OK'."

Pause.

- **Customer:** "I clicked 'Cancel'."
- **Tech Support:** "YOU CLICKED 'CANCEL'???"
- **Customer:** "That's what I was supposed to do, right?"
- **Tech Support:** "No, you were supposed to click 'OK'."
- **Customer:** "I thought you said to click 'Cancel'."
- **Tech Support:** "NO. I said to click 'OK'."
- **Customer:** "Oh."
- **Tech Support:** "Now we have to start over."
- **Customer:** "Why?"
- **Tech Support:** "Because you clicked 'Cancel'."
- **Customer:** "Wasn't I supposed to click 'Cancel'?"
- **Tech Support:** "No. Forget that. Let's start from the top."
- **Customer:** "Ok."

I spent the next fifteen minutes re-constructing the carefully crafted setup for this lady's unique computer.

- **Tech Support:** "All right. Now, are you ready to click 'OK'?"
- **Customer:** "Yes."
- **Tech Support:** "Great. Now click 'OK'."

Pause.

- **Customer:** "I clicked 'Cancel'."

And people wonder why my mouse pad has a target on it labeled "BANG HEAD HERE."

- **Tech Support**: "Hold down the F2 key."
- **Customer**: "Where is that?"
- **Tech Support**: "On the left side of your keyboard, above the two— just right of the Escape key."
- **Customer**: "Ok."
- **Tech Support**: "So now we are in the System Setup screen?"
- **Customer**: "No."
- **Tech Support**: "All right. Hit your Ctrl-Alt-Delete keys. Then your F2 key."
- **Customer**: "Ok."
- **Tech Support**: "Now we are in the System Setup?"
- **Customer**: "No."
- **Tech Support**: "Does it say, 'Loading Windows 95'?"
- **Customer**: "No."
- **Tech Support**: "Can you describe what is on your screen?"
- **Customer**: "It's gray."
- **Tech Support**: "Just gray? It does not say anything?"
- **Customer**: "No. Just gray…with blue and white."
- **Tech Support**: "Are there letters on your screen?"
- **Customer**: "Yes."

Aargh.

- **Tech Support**: "Read them to me."
- **Customer**: "C-o-p-y-r-i—"
- **Tech Support**: "Do they form words? Do the words form phrases? Do the phrases form sentences?"
- **Customer**: "I suppose."

- **Customer**: "I'll have you know, I've never even *seen* a computer before yesterday."

Great. Great start to a call. He wanted to install the Internet connection software we have, so I had him insert the CD. "It ain't workin'!" was all I heard for about two minutes of trying the drive and checking to see if it was really there.

- **Tech Support**: "Sir, could you eject your CD for a moment? We need to check if it's scratched."
- **Customer**: "Ok."
- **Tech Support**: "Look on the bottom of the CD, and see if there are any scratches on it."
- **Customer**: "On the bottom? Shouldn't we check the top?"
- **Tech Support**: "Is the shiny side of the CD on the top?"
- **Customer**: "Of course."
- **Tech Support**: "Ok, could you flip it over so the shiny side is down and then insert it into the drive?"
- **Customer**: "Won't it scratch if I put it in like that?"
- **Tech Support**: "No, it won't scratch."
- **Customer**: "Well, ok...."

He inserted the CD in the drive correctly, and then his computer froze.

- **Customer**: "My computer froze! I told you it would scratch the CD!"
- **Tech Support**: "I'm sure that's not the problem—"
- **Customer**: "I can't believe you scratched the CD."
- **Tech Support**: "Ok, sir, could you hold down 'ctrl' and 'alt', and then—*(clunking sounds)* Hello? Hello, sir?"

There was no one on the line for a moment. Then he spoke up again.

- **Customer**: "I've been holding 'ctrl' and 'alt' for the past two minutes, and nothing is happening at all on my whole damn computer, because you made me scratch the software."

- **Husband**: "Hi. I'm having a problem connecting to the Internet."
- **Tech Support**: "Ok sir, what operating system are you using?"

- **Husband**: "Oh...I'm really not sure...I'm not the computer expert. My wife is. She's sitting at the computer. I'm going to dictate this to her." *(pause)* "She says we use Windows 95."
- **Tech Support**: "Ok. What exactly is the problem?"
- **Husband**: "I can't connect."
- **Wife**: *(in the background)* "We can't even get on—the software is buggy!"
- **Tech Support**: "Ok, what happens when you try to connect?"
- **Husband**: "Ok, the *Connect To:* screen pops up, and it asks for my password."
- **Tech Support**: "Did you put your password in?"
- **Husband**: "Yes, and it keeps asking for it afterwards."
- **Tech Support**: "Do you have your caps lock key on?"
- **Husband**: "Yes, but that shouldn't make any difference."
- **Tech Support**: "Uhm...go ahead and hit the caps lock key until the light goes away."
- **Husband**: "Are you sure? We've always got on with the caps lock key on."
- **Tech Support**: "Yes, I'm sure."
- **Husband**: "Oh, ok. It took my password."
- **Wife**: *(in the background)* "I told you!" *(They start arguing. She takes the phone from him.)* "HELLO?"
- **Tech Support**: "Yes, hello, you should be all set from here."
- **Wife**: "YES HI, I'VE BEEN USING YOUR DAMN SOFTWARE FOR I DON'T EVEN KNOW HOW LONG, AND I STILL CAN'T GET EMAIL FROM MY SON IN THE NAVY!"
- **Tech Support**: "What program do you use for email, ma'am?"
- **Wife**: "I use Windows 95! We already told you that!"
- **Husband**: *(in the background)* "We already told her that, didn't we?"
- **Tech Support**: "No, what mail application...such as 'Eudora', 'Netscape', 'Internet Explorer'..."
- **Wife**: "Microsoft Netscape."
- **Tech Support**: "Netscape?"

- **Wife:** "Yes, 'Microsoft Netscape'."
- **Tech Support:** "Ok, open that up and go to *Options*, and then *Mail and News Preferences*—"
- **Wife:** "No, I want email! I don't want to surf the net!"
- **Tech Support:** "'Netscape' comes with an email program, and we're going to set it up now."
- **Wife:** "Ugh. Fine. Whatever. We'll do it YOUR way."
- **Tech Support:** "Ok." *(explains how to set up popmail)*
- **Wife:** "I'm not getting mail."
- **Tech Support:** "Do you have two phone lines?"

Suddenly I hear the modem attempting to dial in.

- **Tech Support:** *(over the roar of the modem)* "MA'AM? YOU ONLY HAVE ONE PHONE LINE. DON'T TRY TO DIAL IN."

(beep click click)

- **Tech Support:** "You can't dial up with this line. It's already in use."
- **Wife:** "I was always able to use it before YOU changed my settings!"
- **Tech Support:** "No, you will just have to disconn—"
- **Wife:** "You tech support people always mess up my settings, and then I have to bring my computer back to *[retailer]* to get it fixed! You know, you cost me so much money!"
- **Tech Support:** "Ma'am, I didn't change any of your Internet settings."
- **Wife:** "Yes you did, we just went through a NUMBER of things."
- **Tech Support:** "All we did was—"
- **Wife:** "I've had ENOUGH of your service. I'm going back to AOL." *(click)*

This call took more than 45 minutes, in case you wanted to know why there are hold times on support numbers.

- **Customer:** "I haven't had sound for about a month."
- **Tech Support:** "What kind of speakers do you have?"
- **Customer:** "They are stereo."

- **Tech Support:** "Ok, do they plug into the wall?"
- **Customer:** "No."
- **Tech Support:** "So they are the little boxes that don't attach to the monitor?"
- **Customer:** *[angrily]* "Yes."
- **Tech Support:** "Ok, let's see if maybe the speakers are the problem. Do you have a music CD?"
- **Customer:** "Yes."
- **Tech Support:** "Would you go get it?"
- **Customer:** "Sure." *[clunk clunk clunk]* "Do you want one that came with the computer?"
- **Tech Support:** "No, I need a music CD."
- **Customer:** "I think 'The Animals' has music."
- **Tech Support:** "Ok, maybe I am being unclear, I need a regular CD not a CD-ROM—one you buy at a music store."
- **Customer:** "I have a Garth Brooks CD, but I bought it at a swap meet."
- **Tech Support:** "That's great; that CD will work."
- **Customer:** "I go to swap meets all the time to get great deals on stuff. We don't ever go to the music stores."

We get the CD playing with AudioStation, but there's no sound.

- **Tech Support:** "Ok, let's check the volume."
- **Customer:** "I already checked the damn volume when it stopped making sound a month ago!"
- **Tech Support:** "I understand. Let's just double check it real quick."

The volume level turns out ok, and the sound's not muted.

- **Customer:** "I'll just turn it all the way up.... Nope, can't hear a damn thing."
- **Tech Support:** "It looks like you are ok there, now let's check those speakers."
- **Customer:** "Ok, but you might as well replace the whole damn thing right now."

- **Tech Support:** "I'll be happy to replace anything that needs replacing. I just want to make sure we get everything working for you."
- **Customer:** "All right."
- **Tech Support:** "Now those speakers…they are all hooked up? The left connects to the right and then the right connects to the computer?"
- **Customer:** *[obviously without checking]* "Yup."
- **Tech Support:** "Ok. And they are turned off right?"
- **Customer:** "…Listen to me you little…"

I endure a three-minute profanity/threat combo.

- **Customer:** "…Of course they are turned on!! Now you—"
- **Tech Support:** "Whoa, slow down a sec…I *want* you to turn them to the off position, please."

Country music blares. The rest of the conversation takes place shouting over it.

- **Customer:** "Heck son, I don't believe it! What was the problem?"
- **Tech Support:** "The batteries must be dead."

This was my slowest caller ever:

- **Tech Support:** "Thank you for calling; how may I help you?"
- **Customer:** "Ummm…it doesn't work."

Direct and to the point, but just a touch vague. So I prodded him for more information about his problem.

- **Tech Support:** "What does not work?"
- **Customer:** "Ummm…the program doesn't work."
- **Tech Support:** "Could you please be more specific? Was there an error message?"
- **Customer:** "Yes."

I waited a moment, thinking that he would continue on his own. But he didn't.

- **Tech Support:** "And the message was?"
- **Customer:** "Something about a GPF."

- **Tech Support:** "Are you in front of the computer now?"
- **Customer:** "No."
- **Tech Support:** "Can you get in front of the computer?"
- **Customer:** "I guess; let me get out of bed."

Shuffling. Stepping down stairs.

- **Tech Support:** "Are you still there?"
- **Customer:** "Yeah, I have to go downstairs and turn on the computer."

This guy has a 386-25 with 2 megs of RAM loading Windows. It takes about five minutes to boot up his machine.

- **Tech Support:** "Ok, are you in Windows?"
- **Customer:** "Uhhhh…almost…."

Pause.

- **Tech Support:** "Ok, are you in Windows?"
- **Customer:** "Uhhhh…almost…."

Pause.

- **Customer:** "Ok."
- **Tech Support:** "Ok, you are in Windows, can you get into the program for me please?"
- **Customer:** "How do I do that?"
- **Tech Support:** "Just the way you normally do."
- **Customer:** "I don't remember. It's late, and I'm tired. Step me through it."
- **Tech Support:** "Double click on the icon for the program please."
- **Customer:** "Where is that?"

I slowly drop my head to the desk. Finally, I get him to start our application and wait three minutes for the software to load. I'm now fifteen minutes into this call, and I normally average three and a half.

- **Tech Support:** "Ok, can you duplicate the problem for me?"
- **Customer:** "Uhhhhhhhhhhmmmmmmm………no."
- **Tech Support:** "Why not?"
- **Customer:** "I don't remember where it happened."

- **Tech Support:** "I'm afraid I really won't able to help unless I know the error message and where it occurred. You will need to recreate the message and call us back with that information."
- **Customer:** "But I waited so long to talk to you, you people really need to be faster if you expect people to use your service. It takes too long to talk to you. You will lose customers unless you speed it up."
- **Tech Support:** "Thanks for calling, bye-bye."

Customer: "Well, I just want to know if I load this disk into my computer, won't other people be able to get into my computer and access everything I have in there?"
Tech Support: "No, that's not possible."
Customer: "You see it on the TV all the time."

Customer: "Hi, I was wondering if you could fix my laptop. It's under warranty."
Tech Support: "What seems to be the trouble with it?"
Customer: "My wife got mad and threw it in the pool."

Customer: "Can it damage a mouse to be thrown at a wall?"

Ten years ago, I was working for a company selling computerized cash registers. A customer called in to help me with a cash register that didn't connect to the back office computer.

- **Me:** "So, can you tell me the settings of the DIP switches on the cash register?"
- **Customer:** "DIP switch?"
- **Me:** "Oh, sorry, the small switches located on the backside."
- **Customer:** "Eeeerrr…there are no switches there."
- **Me:** "Oh, yes, there are. Right next to the power cord."
- **Customer:** "No. There are no switches. Not any more!"

- **Me:** *(puzzled)* "Huh? Not any more? What do you mean?"
- **Customer:** "Well, you know, my colleague told me that these switches might actually be what caused the problem, so I removed them."
- **Me:** "REMOVED THEM?"
- **Customer:** "Yeah, you know, removed them. With a chisel."

Fact: Boston Computer Museum sells chocolate bars shaped like floppy disks.
Fact: Three-year-old kids see daddy boot his computer using a floppy to play games.
Fact: Computers are *warm* inside…even some quite expensive computers. I don't want to talk about it.

- **Customer:** "About time, too. Are you a real person?"
- **Tech Support:** "Yes sir, how can I help you?"
- **Customer:** "I moved some stuff I don't use to the trash and deleted the trash, and now I'm getting all sorts of %&*#ing errors. What are you going to do about it? You've got an accent, haven't you?"
- **Tech Support:** "Yes sir, I'm in Ireland."

It became apparent that the customer, in his wisdom, had destroyed the Windows registry and deleted just about everything he needed to run Windows.

- **Tech Support:** "Sir, I believe we will have to reload your system with its original operating system, as you are presently unable to get into your system due to the necessary files being deleted. Unfortunately you will lose anything added since you purchased the system. Shall I walk you through the reload sir?"
- **Customer:** "You mean I paid $2,000 dollars, and I have to reload this myself?" *(rants for fifteen minutes, makes death threats and references to being supported by a third world country)* "*&@$ing reload! I'll give you a reload!"
  Bang! Bang!
- **Tech Support:** "Sir, is everything all right?"

- **Customer**: "Sure is. I just blew the $#%&ing thing to bits with my shotgun you *$@%ing &*%$er."
- **Tech Support**: *(taking a satisfying long breath)* "Sir, I would like to advise you at this point that gunshot damage is not covered under the terms and conditions of your warranty. May I suggest a servicer in your locality to assist in the reassembly of your machine?"
- **Customer**: "$%!# you."

One night there was a thunderstorm in the area, and one customer, notorious among the tech support crowd, called:

- **Customer**: "Did you know about the thunderstorm? I heard that I should unplug my computer. Should I do that?"
- **Tech Support**: "In most cases, yes, it is best to at least unplug your phone line. Lightning sometimes causes power surges that can damage your modem."
- **Customer**: "Can it damage other things as well…like the phone?"
- **Tech Support**: "I've never heard of that happening before, but it is a possibility."
- **Customer**: "So do you think that I should unplug the phone from my computer and from all the phones as well?"
- **Tech Support**: *(frustrated)* "Couldn't hurt."
- **Customer**: "So when can I plug them all back in?"
- **Tech Support**: *(really annoyed now)* "When the storm is over."
- **Customer**: "How will I know when it's safe, though?"

My face lit up like a Christmas tree, and it was all I could do to keep myself breathing evenly.

- **Tech Support**: "I will call you."
- **Customer**: "Ok! Thank you!"

- **Tech Support**: "Am I speaking with Mr. Brown?"
- **Customer**: *(in a heavy Italian accent)* "Yesss, who eees this?"

- **Tech Support:** "This is technical support. I see you requested to speak to a 'Mac' expert."
- **Customer:** "And you are theees 'Mac' expert?"
- **Tech Support:** "Yes sir, I am. I see here you're having trouble receiving e-mail—"
- **Customer:** "Yes, your *&@$% company put me on the phone weeeth a stupid woman who didn't know @#$% about 'Macs' and she @#$^ up my compoooota."
- **Tech Support:** "Ok sir, calm down. What specifically is the problem you're having with email?"
- **Customer:** "Cannot you read, stupid woman? Eeeet should say in the teeeecket."
- **Tech Support:** "Sir, if you do not cease using abusive language and profanity, I shall terminate this call immediately."
- **Customer:** *(mocking tone)* "Oooooooh, okay, threatening the customer are we now?"
- **Tech Support:** "Sir, I will repeat my question. What specifically is the problem you are having with email?"
- **Customer:** "Well, every time I go and try to get eeet, it ask me for a pazzword. It never do that before."
- **Tech Support:** "Do you know your password?"
- **Customer:** "Yes."
- **Tech Support:** "Did you enter your password?"
- **Customer:** "No."
- **Tech Support:** *(head in hands)* "Sir, if it is prompting you for a password, you must enter one to receive your email."
- **Customer:** "But, but, but I never deeeed theees before, and it work FINE."
- **Tech Support:** "What email client are you using?"
- **Customer:** "Don't use those big eendustry terms to scaaare me. What is meaning client?"
- **Tech Support:** "What *program* do you use?"

- **Customer**: "'Netscape', I justa download it. I hated that !@#$%@ 'Eudora'."
- **Tech Support**: "Ok sir, I can help you configure 'Netscape' so it won't always ask you for your password, but it *will* ask for it once."
- **Customer**: "But I never enter a #$!@%-ing password before!"

After much cajoling and gratuitous verbal abuse, he finally consented to let me configure his program. He downloaded his mail and then asked, in a sneering tone:

- **Customer**: "So you are the 'Mac' expert, eh?"
- **Tech Support**: "Well, I'm not certified by Apple or anything, but I do own a 'Mac', and I do fine on it."
- **Customer**: "Ok, what ees this 'Mac' TCP DNR file, what does it dooo?"
- **Tech Support**: "Well, the DNR stands for Domain Name Resolver."
- **Customer**: "Eeees that eeeeeeeet?"
- **Tech Support**: "Sir, if you want the specifics on that particular file, I suggest you contact Apple tech support."
- **Customer**: "Some @#$%-ing 'Mac' experta you ar-a, you stupid woman!"
- **Tech Support**: "Sir, I must stress to you that being abusive to technical support can result in the loss of service."
- **Customer**: "Yeah, right-a, som-a stupid woman is-a gonna cancel my account!"
- **Tech Support**: "Consider yourself reported." *(click)*

After that, I received a gushing email from a fellow tech who did a check on the guy a few weeks after the call. By his name and encrypted password was the word "canceled." Sweet.

I work for an entertainment company that has about 150 stores. We run servers in the back office that connect out to dumb terminals that the associates use to ring sales. This is probably the worst call I had to field in two and half years of tech support:

- **Her:** "Umm, My thingies aren't up!"
- **Me:** "Your thingies aren't up?"
- **Her:** "Yes, my thingies aren't up!!"
- **Me:** "Ok, calm down. What exactly are you talking about?"
- **Her:** "The thingies! You know, the thingies that have wires coming out of them!"
- **Me:** "Do you mean the cash registers?"
- **Her:** "I guess."
- **Me:** "Are you talking about the thing that looks like a small TV screen. The place you ring up sales?"
- **Her:** "Yeah! The TV thingies! They aren't up!"
- **Me:** "Ok. What happens when you flip the switch on the front of the monitor?"
- **Her:** "Nothing."
- **Me:** "Are all of your terminals blank? Like they're turned off?"
- **Her:** "Yes. Everything looks turned off."

After ten minutes of checking power cords on one or two of the terminals her manager gets on the phone.

- **Him:** "Why do you have my associate messing with the terminals?"
- **Me:** "Because she called and asked for help."
- **Him:** "Well I don't know who you think you are, but you WILL NOT tell my associates what to do!"
- **Me:** "Well, sir, if you want this problem to get fixed, I'll have to talk to someone."
- **Him:** "No! From now on we'll fix our problems by ourselves, we don't need your help anyway!" *(click)*

Riiiiinnnnnnnggggg....

- **Him:** "Yeah, I need some help. The last idiot I talked to didn't know what he was talking about."
- **Me:** "Well, sir I'll be glad to help."
- **Him:** "Nothing is working."
- **Me:** "Does any of the equipment in the backroom have power?"

- **Him**: "Hold on…. No. Nothing has power. This entire side of town has been blacked out since 3:00am."
- **Me**: "Sir, I need you to take the monitor from terminal 1 and move it to terminal 4, then take terminal 6 and move it to terminal 1."

There is a long wait while he lugs the terminals around. It's not a pleasant task, because of all the dirt and dust that builds up.

- **Him**: "Ok, I'm done. What now?"
- **Me**: "Well, first, I was the 'idiot' you talked to before. Second, a man who doesn't realize that computers need power to work has no real right to comment on someone else's intelligence, does he?"
- **Him**: "Uhh, bahh, uggh." *(click)*

The actual time I spent with the manager on the phone was about twenty minutes. I got written up, but it was worth it.

A support representative friend of mine came up to me one day and said that he thought he had done something wrong. He had been walking a novice 'Mac' user through rebuilding her desktop. She tiresomely questioned every direction the technician made. After half an hour of patiently talking her through what should have been a one-minute process, she finally stated, "Oh! Now it says, 'Are you sure you want to rebuild the desktop on the disk XXX?'"

- **Tech Support**: "Ok—"
- **Customer**: "Oh, now there's something like a spinning barber pole on the screen."
- **Tech Support**: "You didn't press 'OK' did you?"
- **Customer**: "Yes. You said 'OK'."
- **Tech Support**: *(acting alarmed)* "I just said 'Ok,' I didn't mean for you to *press* 'OK'!"
- **Customer**: *(panicking)* "What should I do now?"
- **Tech Support**: "Run! Get out of there! Run! Run!"

The next thing he heard was the phone hitting the floor, the sound of rapidly retreating footsteps and a door slam. After numerous calls over the course of an hour, the customer finally answered the phone. She had waited outside for an hour—when the computer didn't explode, she went back inside and unplugged it.

This is a true account of personal trial, which happened while I was working Tech Support for a company which sold Stock Analysis software. The company would sell data to its customers who would download said data from the company's database on a daily basis. Their listing of data was, therefore, kept on their hard drive, along with the data itself.

- **Me:** "Thank you for calling, how can I help you?"
- **Him:** "Yeah, I want my data back. You need my phone number?"
- **Me:** "Back? What's happened to your data?"
- **Him:** "It's gone. I need it back. Let's get this going, hmmm?"
- **Me:** "Ummm...sir, what happened to it?"
- **Him:** "Don't you worry about *that*. Just give me my freaking data."
- **Me:** "Well, we have several options for data replacement. If you can send us a listing of the stocks you had-"
- **Him:** "Send you a list? I don't have time for this !@*#$!&. Give me my data."
- **Me:** "Uh, unfortunately, it's not that easy. We can—"
- **Him:** "Look, buddy, don't jerk me around. Just press your little whachamajiggers there, zip me down my data, and we're good, ok?"
- **Me:** "Well, sir, these are your options. You can—"
- **Him:** "*$#& you, you stupid &#&$! Stick those options up your @#$*! Why won't you give me my data!?!?"

For the next half hour, I try to explain amidst all the interruptions that he is going to have to pay for the replacement data, either by downloading it again or by getting it on disk from us, and that it would be Monday at the earliest (this was Friday, one hour before closing) before he got it back regardless of which method he chose. This, of course, was unacceptable and resulted in me being subjected to more tirades of ridiculous cursing and genetic analysis. Finally, just to change the subject (he refused to hang up, which I was hoping for), I inquired further into the whereabouts of his missing data.

- **Me:** "Sir, what exactly was it that happened to your data?"
- **Him:** "You have it there! What the hell is in your head?"
- **Me:** "What happened to the data you used to have?"
- **Him:** "Well, this is a new computer, and I need it here, if you morons can handle that."
- **Me:** "Oh! Well, we can transfer it from the old machine. Is it—"
- **Him:** "Nope, nope, can't do that. It's dead."
- **Me:** "Dead?"
- **Him:** "That's right, dead. Your software killed it, so I threw it away."
- **Me:** "You…threw it away? What was wrong with it?"
- **Him:** "What are you, deaf?!? It wouldn't work any more, the monitor, laser printer, nothing, so I threw it all away."
- **Me:** "You threw away the printer?!?"
- **Him:** "Yeah, damn thing cost me $8000 to replace it all, and I'm gonna sue you guys!"
- **Me:** "Well, um, what was wrong with it? Did it get hit by lightning or something?"
- **Him:** "I told you, your software killed it! You got @#!+ in your ears? I put your $#^&*# disk in, and the whole computer just died."
- **Me:** "Died."
- **Him:** "That's right, pooboy!! It wouldn't load anymore, not even windows, just a blank screen with some gobbledygook babble on it."
- **Me:** "What babble was this? An error message?"
- **Him:** "You're damn right, an error message, caused by *your* software!!! I hope you can clean toilets, buddy!"
- **Me:** "Do you have the error message written down somewhere?"
- **Him:** "Well, Mr. Smartypants, as a matter of fact I do! And I'm gonna use it in court to see you in rags!"
- **Me:** "What's it say?"

- **Him:** *(rustle, rustle, curse, curse, mutter)* "Ah hah! Here it is! It says, 'Non System Disk or Disk Error!' You'll pay for this!"

At this point, I, and the other techs who were listening in by now, shared a great laugh, which I didn't bother to mute.

- **Me:** "Sir, you will be happy to know that you threw away a perfectly good $8000 set of machinery because you were stupid enough to leave a disk in the drive."
- **Him:** *(long silence)* "…well, I'm still gonna sue you guys…"
- **Me:** "I want front row seats in the courtroom. Have a nice evening." *(click)*

Epilogue: When he called back on Monday, the manager terminated his account for abusive behavior for that record two minutes, thirty-eight second call.

Customer: "I've been signed up with your service for over a week, and have not been able to connect even once because of busy signals. If I can't get any better service than that, I'm going to switch to another ISP."

Tech Support: "Hmmm…that shouldn't be happening. We're no where near maxing out our dial up lines. Are you sure you're dialing the right number?"

Customer: "I'm not stupid! I know my own phone number!"

Tech Support: "Now click the 'connect' button."

Customer: *(modem dialing noises)* "Hold on, I have another call." *(pause)* "Hmmm. No one there. Ok, I'll try this again." *(modem dialing noises)* "Hold on, I got another call." *(pause)*

- **Customer:** "I need help with this dialer. The police have already shown up to my office twice today."
  Police? Ok, whatever.
- **Tech Support:** "Ok, let's check out the settings. Do you have anything entered for getting an outside line?"
- **Customer:** "A nine."
- **Tech Support:** "Do you need to dial a 9 for an outside line?"

- **Customer**: "I'm not sure. I think so."
- **Tech Support**: "Could you double check?"
- **Customer**: "Sure. *(pause)* Nope. Turns out we don't need it."
- **Tech Support**: "Ok. Then remove it. What do you have for the area code?"
- **Customer**: "One and then [area code]."
- **Tech Support**: "Uhm, you don't need the one. Windows 95 automatically adds that."
- **Customer**: "Oh. So you mean…"
- **Tech Support**: "Yes, your computer was dialing 911 and then the phone number."

Customer: "I can't log in to my account."
Tech Support: "Ok, let's look at your configuration."
Customer: "Ok…but I know that my User ID is case sensitive."
Tech Support: "Yes it is. Ok, what does it say in the 'User ID' field?"
Customer: "'Case Sensitive'."

Tech Support: "I'm sorry ma'am, but you'll have to register before using the service."
Customer: "Really? Well, I tried. I mean, I answered all the questions. It was a little noisy but I answered all the questions."
Tech Support: "Noisy? How could it be noisy? Your modem dialed, connected, and brought up the questions, right? Then what did you do?"
Customer: "I picked up the phone and answered everything on the screen. There was a lot of static, but I figured they could still hear me."

Half a year ago a customer sent in a message saying that he wanted another email address, and he wanted to know how much it would cost. I replied that customers were allowed up to five for no added charge. All I needed was a name and a password for each account. I have changed the names in the following exchange to protect the idiotic.

- **Customer:**

  Oh, then I would like Jane Doe for my wife, John Doe for my son, Jennifer Doe for my daughter. I'll ask them what passwords they want and send you another message.

- **Me:**

  I'm sorry, in my earlier email I was not very clear. I apologize for any confusion. I will try to be very clear in this message so that there will not be any problems, but if you do have any, you can always call.

  All email addresses must be between four and twenty characters. A character is any lower case letter, number, the dash or–, and the underscore or–. You CANNOT use any spaces or other special characters. The same rules apply for your password.

  Here are some examples to help you in your selection.
  The usernames of: Jane Doe, John Doe, Jane_Doe, and John_Doe are NOT usable because of the capital letters and the spaces.
  These would be fine: janedoe, johndoe, jenniferdoe
  Or you could use: jane_doe, john_doe, jennifer_doe

  If you wanted something shorter, you would need to use middle initials since your first initials all start with the same letter. For example, if your son's middle initial was "p" you could use: jpdoe
  Their first names would normally be another good alternative, but someone else already has "john". So you could use "jane" and "jennifer" but NOT "john". "johnny" has also been used, but "jonathan" has not.

  Do you have any further questions? If this is not clear to you, you can call during office hours and ask for me, or call after hours and get whoever is on 24-hour tech support.

- **Customer:**

  I think I have it now. How about this:
  jane, with the password of as4you*
  bunny, with the password of ^to^

johnny, with the password of astronaut!
Are those okay?

- **Me:**

    As I said in my last message, there are no special characters allowed, so the passwords given are not usable. Just so we are clear, when I say special characters, I mean ~!@#$%^&*()+=`[]{};:'",.<>/and?. NONE of these can be in the username OR password.

    Also, you cannot use "johnny" because someone already has it. If you can get me usable passwords for "jane" and "bunny" I will put them in the system immediately. Then we will only have to worry about your son.

- **Customer:**

    Oh. Now I get it. Then I want to use these:
    jane doe with the password of supermom kitten with the password of kitten, unless they can't be the same, then I'll use daughter starranger with the password of blaster
    Can you tell me how to set those up?

- **Me:**

    I put "starranger" in the system with the password you listed. The instructions on this page are how to set up the extra email accounts on your computer: *(url)*

    If you have ANY trouble with this, or if ANY error occurs, call out help line. The number is xxx-xxxx. All of us can help you with setting up these email addresses. Just print out this message and have it with you when you call. This is a 24-hour tech support line. In fact, I suggest you call and let us lead you through it step by step over the phone. It will be much easier. The bad news is there is still a problem with the other two addresses. "kitten" is being used by someone else already, and I can not put in "jane doe" because of the space.

In case you still wanted them, I did put in "jane" with the password of "supermom" and "bunny" with the password of "daughter". Are those okay?

- **Customer:**

    I don't know what is happening! I set up johnny, with the password of astronaut, just like the instructions said, and it always gives me an error saying that the password is bad! What is wrong! I don't want to try and set up kitten and jane till you tell me what is wrong.

- **Me:**

    Sir, as I stated in my earlier email, johnny is not available.
    Why don't you call the 24 hour tech support line so we can work this out faster than through email? Believe me, it will be easier.

- **Customer:**

    I CAN'T CALL THE HELP LINE!
    I don't get home till you are closing! There won't be anyone in the office!
    I WANT to do this over the phone but CAN'T because you close so early!

- **Me:**

    Sir, as said many times before, this is a 24-hour help line. Even though we are only in the office from 9am to 6pm, the help line pages us. In fact, this week is **my** rotation with the pager so any time from now till Sunday you can speak with me. This will be to your advantage since I'm familiar with the situation.

- **Customer:** *(sent to my boss, then forwarded to me)*

    I have sent several email messages to your tech support and received NO REPLIES!
    All I want is a few additional email addresses, and I learned from your site that I can get four more for free. But when I send email to the technical address, I get no answers.
    Can you help me?

- **Me:** *(to my boss)*
    He is lying through his teeth. Here are his letters and my replies. *(I included the emails here)*
- **My Boss:**
    Okay. I'll call him.

That was the end of the email exchange for a while. My boss called the man and asked him if he had ever gotten any replies from the tech mail address. The customer denied that he had. So my boss read him one of my replies and asked if the customer had gotten it. He denied that he had, so my boss read him his next email and asked why he was replying to mail he never got.

The man then broke down and explained that he was:

- Confused by my telling him that some names were not available.
- Could not call the tech support line since it was only open on the weekdays during office hours.
- Found the instructions on our site too confusing.
- My boss then spent over *three hours* on the phone leading the man through setting up the other email accounts.

The next day the man called tech support to complain that he had changed the mail accounts to "johnny", "jane doe", and "kitty" and that they had stopped working, so he was going to call on the weekend to have us help him again. He never called back about the email.

Three months later, his computer broke down, and he brought it to the shop. I worked on the machine. He had "uninstalled" some software by deleting the directories and then wondered why the computer would not boot up. He remembered seeing many of the programs putting things into the "windows" directory, so he had deleted as much of that as he could. Miraculously, re-installing Windows fixed his machine. When he came in to pick up the machine, I asked about the other email addresses. He said they were too much trouble for him, and that he just started using hotmail instead. I told him that that was probably a better choice for him.

But it gets better.

Throughout the next five months, we had no less than two calls a month from this man. His settings, including the DNS numbers, email addresses, home page, and so on, would mysteriously change. He blamed viruses, his kids, the weather, and everything but himself.

One day he called to cancel. He explained that his son was moving away to college and would have access there, and so since his Internet access had only been for his son, he would no longer need it. We threw a small office party after he hung up. We shredded his account on the server and sighed a great sigh of relief. Three days later he came in with a laptop. He wanted his account back.

Apparently he had terminated his account because his son was taking the computer with him to college. But this guy's job, "a sensitive job with the federal government," required him to have Internet access from home, and apparently it had been this way all along. His boss had apparently asked him what was going on when email to him suddenly started bouncing. So he was supplied with a laptop so he could continue working at home.

We setup the laptop for his account, and he took it and went home. Less than an hour later, he called. He had changed his access phone number, his primary DNS number, his WINS numbers (which we don't even use), his password, his email server names, and his email address, and had put a password on the laptop that he did not remember.

We fixed it over the phone. The whole time he denied having changed anything but admitted to "checking on the settings." It took over two hours.

We are hoping for an act of nature, or that he will get fired and they will take back the laptop.

Customer: "I get this error when I check my mail. It says, 'There are no new messages.'"
Tech Support: "How may I help you?"
Customer: "I'm writing my first email."
Tech Support: "Ok, what seems to be the problem?"

Customer: "Well I can get the 'a'. But how do I put the circle around it?"

Tech Support: "This is technical support returning your call for support. How can I help you?"
Customer: "I want to lodge a complaint."
Tech Support: "What seems to be the problem?"
Customer: "I specifically asked you *not* to program my Internet with pornography. I want it removed immediately."

Tech Support: "What operating system are you running?"
Customer: "Pentium."

Customer: "I have a teer to teer network."
Customer: "I have a scummy card in my system."
Customer: "I lost my blue cyanide color."
Customer: "I have a cursing flasher."
Customer: "I ran Microwave Defrost, but it didn't help."
(Referring to 'Microsoft' Defrag.)
Customer: "I have Microsoft Exploder."
Customer: "I have Microscope Exploiter."
Customer: "I have Netscape Complicator."
Customer: "I have Netscape Regulator."
Customer: "Uhh…I have Newscape and Outlook Exposure."
Customer: "I use Outlook Explorer."

- **Customer:** "My computer won't start up."
- **Tech Support:** "Is the power light on?"
- **Customer:** "Yes."
- **Tech Support:** "Is anything on the monitor?"

Customer: "Yes, it says to press F2 for setup, or I can press F1 and fill out a resume."

IDIOT WATCHERS

A tech support call usually starts with a whiny "Help! I can't get online!" To establish why, I must go through the customer's settings, line by painful, tormented line. They are required only to listen, follow my direction, and read what they see on the screen. I, on the other hand, must grind my teeth, repeat myself four and five times, give basic vocabulary lessons, and struggle desperately not to weep openly or kick office furniture. I usually begin with a simple question, "Are you running Windows 95 or 98?" I've had some really cracked replies: "No, AOL", "Microsoft Something", "Windows 97", and the best one of all, the Customer who said she had Windows 94:

Support: "That's not possible, Win 94 doesn't exist. Is it 95 or 98?"
Customer: "It doesn't exist? Does that mean I can't get Internet?"
Support: "No, it just can't be 94. It's probably 95 or 98. I can show you how to check…"
Customer: "I live on Main Street."
What do you do with that?!

Then there was the lady that responded, "Oh, dear, I don't know anything about my computer…all I know is that I have the one that looks like a VCR. I don't have the round one. It's the one that looks like the VCR. Is that what you need to know?" Um, not exactly. Next they are asked to open the Control Panel. Or at least they used to be, until someone asked me if he needed a screwdriver for that. I told him that he just needed to click on the Start Button and Settings, and he told me he didn't see anything like that…all he saw was this big box…So I tried "Let's go to My Computer" on the next one…and got "Now, how am I supposed to get to your computer when I can't get online?" These are the same type of people who call and ask me if I can see what they're doing when they're not connected…they type a user name and then pause, and ask "Is that right? Did I type it right? Oh, you can't see what I'm typing?" While going through the settings, you can sometimes start to draw out what really happened. "Well, my nephew's cousin's sister-in-law's brother's boyfriend's uncle by marriage was over last night, and he was trying to program my hard drive to get V.90." Great. "But you told me you hadn't made any changes to your system." "Oh, no, I haven't. All the icons are still on my desktop."

ARRRGGH!!!

Editor's Note: Be sure to visit this website at http://www.idiotwatchers.com. You'll find the stories very amusing—I guarantee it.

Dodo Award Winners:

These awards have been presented throughout the years. Here are a few of the best ones…

Today's dodo called Tech Support to solve a "Cannot-open-page" type of error message coming up as soon as her browser opened, every time she logged in. Our tech had her check her Home Page setting in her Internet Properties. Lo and behold, this rocket scientist had typed her street address on the URL line for her Home Page!

Today's dodo called with some questions about our company's Internet Service. One of them was, "Is the Internet Microsoft compatible?"

When asked to choose a letter of the alphabet between P and X, today's dodo distinguished herself by choosing M. Upon finding out that she was headed for the Daily Dodo, she remarked, "Oh, that's not really an idiot thing—that's just me."

Conversation overheard in a restaurant:
Dodo: What's a dot com, anyway?
Boob: I don't know–is it a cruise?

A user called their job's support center after a power outage to ask, "I was working in Excel when the power went out, can you retrieve my document for me?" Of course the tech asked if the loser had saved before the power out, only to receive the dodo answer, "No...."

An ISP Tech had answered the phone with the usual "How can I help you?" The customer very politely inquired as to how to setup his Internet service. The tech dutifully walked him through the setup, only to reach the end and have the customer ask, "Excuse me, I got everything you said, but what is a click?"

Today's long overdue dodo award goes to all those individuals who seem bright by already having a User ID and password chosen and ready when they call to set up a new Internet account, then blow it by proudly announcing, "I use that same User ID and password for EVERYTHING! It's much easier to remember that way." D'oh! Thanks for the tip...

Calling for tech support, today's dodo gave our Primary Name Server's IP Address as his account number....

Winner of today's dodo award is the clueless wonder who said that the .zip extension meant that the files were encrypted...hello, have we ever heard of compression?!

Today's dodo wanted to know which was the better browser, Yahoo or Netscape...—

I got a call from a dodo today who said he was "going to school for computers". He went on to say, "I'm trying to boot up and my screen says 'Non-System Disk or Disk Error'. What do I do? Does that mean my hard drive is bad?"

Checking for idiocy in the wild, I recently called 1-800-DUMB-ASS, just to see what would happen. Today's Dodo Award goes to the Marketing Company that answered!

Today's dodo, after talking on the phone to a particularly infuriating customer, vented by hurling the receiver across the room…only to have it recoil at the end of the cord and hit him square in the forehead!

I told a new customer that the user name for their Internet Account had a limit of eight characters, and the dodo asked me, "You mean like eight different people?"

Today's dodo, when discussing getting Internet Service, said, "This is all new to me—I'm from Philadelphia." We all know there's no Internet Access out there in the sticks…

The gentleman who called me to say that his computer was stopping halfway through boot-up made the dodo list for asking whether the Internet was slow or the site busy and causing this problem.

New Accounts #2: Setup Instructions

Where were we? Ah, yes. New Accounts.

So the (internet) account is all set up. All they have to do is configure their system. This is done using a two or three page packet of Step-by-Step Instructions written by me and/or my predecessors. This is a whole lot easier said than done.

The first challenge comes in getting them the packet. They don't want to use snail-mail, and I am VERY reluctant to do a phone setup (40 minutes of indescribable hell), so I usually ask, "What is the fastest way I can get you the Setup Packet?" Most often they ask me for suggestions, in which case I ask them if they either have a fax machine or an existing e-mail account that I can use to send them, or if they would like to stop by our office and pick them up.

I receive a variety of answers:

"Yes, I have a fax machine." "Great, what's the number?" "Oh, I don't know how to work it. It's in my computer."

"You can e-mail them to me." "Great, what's the address?" "Didn't you just give me one?" Now why on Earth would I send setup directions to your account if you can't get in to get the directions to get in? It's a Catch-22 from hell. I should have e-mailed them to her to see how long she would have waited for them to arrive.

And another real winner asked if I could put them on a floppy disk for him. I explained that I could, but there was no need, as they were written…and even if I did, I would still need to find some way to get the disk to him!

Another told me to mail them and when I said I would, asked me how I would know his address. That was one of those that had me doubting myself—looking down at the application to see if I had indeed just asked him for it. "Uh, you just gave it to me?" "That's right, I did. Duh."

You said it, so I didn't have to…

An Idiot By Any Other Name

As promised, this is the sad tale of the worst "I can't get my e-mail" call I have ever received. It is also my first Idiot call, the one that inspired me to start the list. I think I have shoes smarter than this woman. (Names, as usual, have been changed.)

A few months ago (back when I was new(er) at this and had NO idea what I was getting into), I received a call that started the usual way.…

<RING><RING> "Good morning, may I help you?"

The caller stated her User ID and problem in the same sentence. We seemed to be off to a good start. Some calls take more than a little while just to get that much information. She couldn't get her e-mail. We went through the usual battery of questions, and I discovered without too much trouble that she was using Netscape on a Windows 95 machine. I sent her a test message and she said she didn't get it. We spent some 20 minutes walking through the settings at an agonizing level of detail. "I want you to right click…No, don't open it…RIGHT click…That's with the right mouse button…okay, the one you don't normally click with.… Yes, close it up.… Then right click.… Oh, that's okay, just close it again.… Now we are ready to right click.…"

Finding all the settings correct, I then sent her another test message, to which she replied, "Yes, it's here, so is the other one."

Awk-Pfft! Daring to ask why she had made me go through the settings with her if she had received my original test message (and nevermind why she said she didn't get it) made me wish I hadn't. It turned out that she just wanted to make sure they were correct, never realizing that if they were not, she would never have been able to retrieve the first test message. ASSuming that all was now well in her world, I tried (foolish mortal) to end the call. She stopped me. "But that's not the problem." For the first time ever during a call, I was afraid.

"Then what is the problem?"

"Well, I have a PC and a Mac. It's the Mac that I can't get my e-mail on." D'OH!!!! I whacked myself in the forehead hard enough that I think I gave myself a concussion. That is the only way to explain how I ever made it through the rest of the call. <Grumble> "Wasted half an hour <grumble> on a machine that wasn't the problem" <snort, stomp, grumble>…. <Saccharine sweet phone voice dripping with venom> "Okay, shall we fire up the Mac, then?"

While she was booting up the Mac, my life was flashing before my eyes. I still have never seen a Mac before in my life and that call was the first time I had ever been obligated to assist a Mac User. I was planning to bluff. Fortunately, I was saved by the fact that she was using Netscape. Netscape I could handle. I even knew what her problem was. There is a setting in most mail readers offering you the option to either copy your mail from the remote server to your machine and leave a copy of it on the server, or copy it and delete it from the server. She was of course copying it on to the Windows PC and then deleting it off, which would explain why she wasn't finding it when she went in with the Mac to look for it. It had already been deleted. Oh, clever one…I was pleased. It was short-lived.

So we drag ourselves painfully back to the Windows PC to look at the setting in question only to find that it is already set to leave her messages on the server after copying them. Drat! Damn! I was so sure that is what it was…So I had to sorrowfully inform her that we had to walk through the settings on the Mac. Worse yet, I had no clue what could be wrong. Forty minutes, now, I have been on the phone with this lady.

I chose to tackle the "hard" settings first…Server Types. They were correct. Then the easy ones, Identity. That is where you put your name and e-mail address. The e-mail address was correct, but she had left the section for "Your Name" blank. Before I could tell her that the "Your Name" setting had nothing to do with the problem, she had uttered the immortal words: "What goes on that line?" Now, a blank line with "Your Name" in front of it…what could go there? I figured maybe she wasn't sure whether to put her real name or User ID….

I explained that the "Your Name" line was for whatever she wanted to appear on the "From" line on her messages. She asked me what the "From" line was. Now this was getting ridiculous. I told her to just put her name on the blank line, however she wanted it to appear in her messages. She asked me to explain that better for her. With my head on my desk and my hands over my eyes, I explained that anything she wanted could go there. Just her first name, or her first and last name, or a nickname, or just Mrs. So-And-So. "So if I just wanted my first name to show in the messages, then I would put Mary, right?"

My mouth doesn't always send a request to the tact department before it speaks. It's very independent that way. I've got to watch it every minute, or else it will say things like "Well, if your first name is Mary, then that will work great for you. I'd have to say it wouldn't work as well for me." That name rang a bell, though. I was sure I had seen it somewhere recently. She said "Oh" and giggled a little. Then we were ready for another test. I sent the message and waited for her to receive it. She did not. Everything was set up correctly, and she was actually connected to the Internet. (I get many calls from those who are not.)

I don't know what clued me, but clear out of the blue, I asked if she had clicked "Get Message".

"Clicked what?"

<Through clenched teeth> "Top left hand corner…says "Get Message" on it…Click it…"

"Oh, yes, you're right, here they all are…Thank you very much…CLICK!" Fastest hang up I had ever seen.

After that call, while therapeutically sharing the highlights with the rest of the office, I remembered where I had seen that name before…on a special list of IDIOTS that my predecessor had left for me as a warning of who to avoid dealing with at any length….

Tech Support Calls Installment #1

And now we get to what this list is really about…the idiot calls I get all day long. I sit at a desk all day, waiting to help people who can't operate their computers. That in and of itself is not a bad thing. After all, if some first generation computer programmers (read: hackers) hadn't decided back right around the time when I was still having tea parties with my Frankenstein and Wolfman dolls (yes, I was a twisted child) to bring computers to the masses, I wouldn't know how to use one either…so I don't mind helping the people who have a problem and genuinely want to learn and solve it. The people with a clue. The ones that can think, but just haven't learned about these wonderful machines yet.

It's the IDIOTS that get to me…the ones that think the VCR is part of the dog or that it should automatically do their bidding because they are human and they are smarter than it is. Like the ones that assume automatically that they are doing it right and something must be wrong on the other end or the ones that can't understand the best and worst thing about working with computers: that they do EXACTLY what they are told, no more, no less…those are the ones that get to me. And I would like to share them with you. (If you don't get one of the jokes, e-mail me and I'll turn it into a neat little analogy for you…then post it on a future list. Moohahahaha…)

<RING><RING> "Good morning/afternoon, May I help you?"

And so an idiot call begins. Sometimes I know right off I've got a live one; other times I am halfway through the call before my IQ points start slipping away. (Names have been changed to protect the un-enlightened.) I dread the type of call that begins...

<RING><RING> "Good morning/afternoon, May I help you?"

Yes, I'm having some trouble...I can't get online...Yes, that's right, I can't connect at all...

One lady, after setting up her account with our two-and-a-half page setup packet, called to say she tried to get online, but was getting Invalid User name and Password. Okay, so I confirm her User ID and password, and have her try to log in while I watch from our side. The screen that registers each outside logon never moved, telling me her call was never reaching our server. So how could our server be rejecting her User ID and password, if her call was never even reaching it? I called her back and asked why she had not tried to connect.

"But I did, and it said it again."

"Said what again?"

"About invalid."

"Okay, please tell me EXACTLY what the error message said."

"It said the name I put in was invalid."

"It may help if I know exactly what the message was—in the words the computer uses—so I can figure out what we are doing wrong."

Hard learned lesson: If it is avoidable, do not state explicitly to the customer that THEY ALONE are doing something wrong, especially when they are. Don't say it is your side when it is not, but you will annoy them and make them feel silly (heavens, why ever would they feel that way?) if you even imply that they are dopey. It is rough, but in the long run, it pays to tactfully take a little credit for their misdeed.

"Okay, I tried it again and it said: 'Prodigy Code Invalid'. See, your system doesn't like the user name you gave me." By this time I have the phone cord wrapped around my neck and am begging one of my co-workers to pull it tight for me.

I choke out, "'Prodigy' code? You called 'Prodigy'?"

Now she puts her husband on the line, who says, "You mean this isn't 'Prodigy'? I thought it was ON-LINE (pronounced like two words) service...what is it, then? <Company Name>? What's <Company Name>? Are you connected with 'Prodigy'? Oh...Mary, that's why...we're calling the wrong place. Thanks...now how do I fix it?"

ARGH!!!!

<RING><RING> "Good morning/afternoon, May I help you?"

"Yes, I'm having some trouble...I can't get online...Yes, that's right, I can't connect at all...It still keeps taking me right to 'AOL'. I just switched over to your service today and worked through the setup packet." I am the clever tech supporter (like an athletic supporter, only better paid?) and with this first sentence, I have figured out her problem. She didn't change the setting that tells her computer which dialer to bring up (which phone number to dial to get to the Internet). She is still using 'AOL's dialer and trying to connect to our service. Oh, I am clever. (You've got to know this is going somewhere...)

So...I explain to her what is happening (because I am so clever and have figured it out already and don't need to ask for any more details about the problem) and advise her on which setting to adjust to fix it. Together (tech support has lots of bonding involved) we go to her Control Panel to change the appropriate setting...and it is already correct. A whistle is heard in the distance and flaming debris from the crash of my ego lands all over my desk. I make a sound like Bill the Cat in the old Bloom County comics: Awk-Pffft! Okay, think fast...what else could it be? Are you clicking on the 'AOL' icon instead of the 'Internet Explorer' icon? No. Are your other settings correct? After a 10-minute walk-through of the pertinent settings...Yes, they are. We pause while I ponder. I ask her to try it again. I hear modem sounds. "Nope, it has still connected me to AOL. I have their homepage up right here." A dim clue light flickers in the distance, like a lone lighter at a concert...It is beginning to come to me, and I don't know which of us at this point is the bigger of two idiots.

"Their homepage is up? Homepage? Do you see two little computers connected to each other down by your clock? Double click that for me, please…"

"It says Connected to <Our Service>…Connected at…"

She hadn't changed the page her browser automatically went to at startup, making her an idiot for not knowing the difference between a start page and a dialer…but somehow I think I was the bigger bunghole for ASSuming she was having a dialer problem and not checking the OBVIOUS first…instead I spent twenty minutes trying to get her off 'AOL' when a three-command check on my side would have told me she was already connected with us and not 'AOL'….

You see what I mean by the IQ points slipping away…

Tech Support Calls Installment #2

Greetings and welcome to the second installment of Tech Support Calls. If I recall correctly (and I always recall correctly), we were discussing the "I can't get…" whiners. So many times during the day I am well on the way to a halfway sensible thought process when suddenly, a savage RRRI-IIINNNNGGGG!!!! shatters my tiny clue…

<RING><RING> "Good morning/afternoon, May I help you?"

"Hello? Yes, I have a problem. I can't seem to get my e-mail."

Oh, my favorite kind. I push my chair against the wall and prop my feet up on the desk. These are usually long.

"Okay…what's your username again?" I try to say that at least once a call, in true BOFH tradition. They never get it, which is almost all of the fun. (You, too, may pay homage to the Bastard Operator From Hell at http://www.iinet.net.au/~bofh/ or http://www.plig.net/bofh/) Not that I need to ask for the username, I can tell most of our boneheads by first name and degree of cluelessness.

After the username, I generally try to get all the pertinent information. Standard questions follow, with worst-ever answer in parentheses:

Are you online right now? (Well, I'm sitting in front of the computer.)
Which operating system are you using? (Uh, it's a computer. I don't know.)
(Deciding the above was too vague, I switched to "Are you using Windows
95?" and once got "No, Windows 97." Where the hell do you go from
there?!)
Okay, have you set up your mail reader? (No.) or (What's a mail reader?)
Which mail reader are you using? (Windows 95)
Okay, let's start by opening your mail reader. Double click your browser
icon. (We don't want "My computer", do we?")

After the basics are out of the way, we can start double-checking the
settings. This usually consists of me telling them where to go
(Moohahahahahaaa, don't I wish?) and them reading to me what they
have typed in as their settings. Important settings include server name
(name of computer on our side that stores their mail, provided by me at
sign up) and username and password (provided by them at sign up). You
would not believe how agonizingly long this takes. There are days I would
rather have teeth pulled.

I had one lady looking for the word "Servers" on her menu and just not
finding it, despite the fact that I KNEW it was there...we searched and
searched, until she finally stopped saying "But I just don't have that" and
asked condescendingly, "Do you mean SERVICES? That's on this
menu..." I asked her to spell it out for me, and she self-righteously spelled
"S-E-R-V-E-R-S"...

The e-mail address is often a source of distress to the clueless. They are
told at sign up to give me the e-mail name they want and their instruction
packet supplies everything after the @. One classic bonehead called for help
getting her mail. I checked, and the account had been created the previous
day. Walking her through the settings, I discovered that for e-mail address, she
had put in something other than the one I had given her. The domain wasn't
even right. Instead of so_and_so@ourdomain.com, this winner had some-
thing_else@made_up_domain.com. I corrected it and she was annoyed. "I

thought you said the e-mail name could be anything I wanted…" Yes, bozo, that was BEFORE you chose one!

Occasionally, there is one that has a genuine problem, where the program that reads their mail is actually corrupted, which means they have to remove (uninstall) the program and re-install it. Telling one special caller that she had to uninstall the program prompted her to ask me, "Oh, uninstall the software…do you mean go to the website?" That's like, "Oh, change the tire…do you mean paint the roof?"

CLASSICS

Here are some of the best classics I could find on the Internet. You may recognize a few of them but they're still funny as hell. Contributors include HarryC, Digital Helpdesk, SiliconGlen, Yuckitup and ShadowStorm. Enjoy!

Did I Screw Myself?

Customer: I just canceled my account with 'AOL' because their modem kept hanging up on me, and I want to see if you guys have any better service.
Tech: What kind of modem do you have, Sir?
Customer: Well I bought the cheapest 28.8 modem I could find.
Tech: Well Sir, when you buy the cheapest 28.8 modem you can find, what you get is the cheapest 28.8 modem that can be made, and frequent disconnects are a re-occurring problem with cheap 28.8 modems.
Customer: Hmmm…. Did I screw myself?
Tech: It doesn't look good, Sir.

Why Techs Should Not Read While Talking

One of our techs admitted a somewhat embarrassing screw up on his part. Late one night, about thirty minutes prior to closing, things were getting slow and the calls coming in to Tech Support had tapered off. This particular tech began browsing one of the erotic news groups when he found a rather interesting post. After a few minutes of reading he had become submersed in the tale being told. About that time the phone rang and it was a customer. The tech began trouble shooting the customer's problem, yet still reading the erotic tale at the same time. Well, do you know how some people read out loud without even realizing it? This tech made that mistake for a split second.

Tech: "Do you touch yourself?"
Customer: "What?!"
Tech: *<Realizing he has goofed, he attempts to recover>* "Ummmm...Did you get a touch error?" *<No such error>*
This was about all the tech would admit to.

Sometimes Customers Diagnose Their Own Problem

Tech: Internet Tech Support, this is so-and-so speaking. May I have your username please?
Customer: Yes I'm having problems staying connected to the Internet. I can connect to the Internet just fine, but after just a few minutes I get disconnected. Are you having any problems?
Tech: No Ma'am. Everything is working fine as far as I know. Lets look over your modem settings and make sure everything is ok.
Customer: Ok, where do you want to start?
Tech: Well, first click on START/SETTINGS and then CONTROL PANEL.
Customer: Ok. I'm clicking on START...then SETTINGS...then... <click!–several touch-tones are heard>
Customer: Cindy! I'm on the phone!
Cindy: Mom! I need to call Tiffany!
Customer: Well you'll have to wait! I'm on the phone with Internet Tech Support.
<Cindy hangs up the phone>
Customer: Sorry, that was my daughter. Ok where were we?
Tech: Ok, click on START/ SETTINGS/ CONTROL PANEL and then MODEMS.

Customer: Ok...START...then SETTINGS...CONTROL PANEL...and MODEMS...<Click!–several touch tones heard>
Customer: Cindy! I'm ON THE PHONE!
Cindy: Well hurry up! <SLAM!>
Customer: I'm sorry Sir. Ok, I'm in MODEMS now.
Tech: Ok, now click on the DIAGNOSTICS tab at the top.
Customer: Ok.
Tech: How many COM ports do you have showing?
Customer: Well COM 1 says, "No modem installed, and COM 2 says no modem..." <click! several touch tones heard>
Customer: CINDY! Get off the phone this minute!
Cindy: <SLAM!>
Customer: Sir...
Tech: Yes?
Customer: I think I know what my problem is. Thank you. <click>

Sega Internet

Me: Ok Ma'am what operating system are you running?
Cust: Operating system?
Me: Yes, is it 'Win 95', '3.1', a 'Mac'? That's what I need to know.
Cust: No, no, none of that.
Me: Then...what are you using to connect?
Cust: Oh, my 'Sega Saturn'.
(After hitting the mute button and bursting out laughing, I quickly composed myself and tried to keep from laughing from that point on)
Cust: Can you help me please?
Me: Ok, first off, what are you trying to do?
Cust: Well, I first wanted to get my email. I have a friend who bet me $200 he could beat me at 'Mortal Kombat'.
(Another pause with the mute button)

Me: I'm sorry Ma'am but we do not support the 'Sega Saturn Link', as far as I know you should not be able to connect to us with it at all.

Cust: So you are telling me that because of you guys I will lose $200.

Me: Not really, just that you cannot do it through us.

Cust: Who do you think I am, Donald Trump?! I can't go out and buy a computer to use the Internet at all...I'm gonna lose my money because you refuse to help me?

Me: I'm sorry Ma'am but we do not support 'Saturn'. I suggest you call 'Sega' and....

Cust: Listen here you f***** as*****!! I don't need to hear what YOU think; you have to help me NOW!

(At this point I couldn't help but laugh)

Cust: You think you are really fresh aren't you? I want your name.

(By now I knew that the situation would never reach a solution, so I let myself go)

Me: My name Ma'am? Oh, yes my name Is Sonic...Hedgehog...that's S, O, N...

Cust: You guys will hear from me!!! (CLICK!)

Needles to say, she then emailed our support department, claiming some wise guy calling himself Sonic Hedgehog was rude and refused to help her with her 'Sega Saturn' connection. She received a courteous response saying we couldn't help her. She then tried calling tech support several times asking for different techs each time but never got through. We eventually got her phone number and had the Dept. Head of Technical Support call her and request she stop calling tech support.

A man purchased a laptop from me. He called about a week later and said that it would no longer boot-up. I tried to troubleshoot with him about what went wrong but he said it wouldn't even start. I had him bring it in and I couldn't get it to work either. I was making preparations to remove the hard drive so I could put it into a new laptop for him. When I turned it over, I saw 16 nicely drilled holes in the bottom of the case. I asked him how this had happened and he said that it was getting hot sitting on his lap all the time, so he drilled some air holes in it. "Could that be the problem?" he asked.

Caller: I think my computer doesn't know what it is doing.
Tech: (Pause) Why? What is the problem with the system?
Caller: Well, it keeps asking me "What is this?"

ASSET BARCODE

At our company we have asset numbers on the front of everything. They give the location, name, and everything else just by scanning the computer's asset barcode or using the number beneath the bars.
Customer: "Hello. I can't get on the network."
Tech Support: "Ok. Just read me your asset number so we can open an outage."
Customer: "What is that?"
Tech Support: "That little barcode on the front of your computer."
Customer: "Ok. Big bar, little bar, big bar, big bar..."

CAPITAL LETTERS

This guy calls in to complain that he gets an "Access Denied" message every time he logs in. It turned out he was typing his username and password in capital letters.
Tech Support: "Ok, let's try once more, but use lower case letters."
Customer: "Uh, I only have capital letters on my keyboard."

F1 FOR HELP

My friend was on duty in the main lab on a quiet afternoon. He noticed a young woman sitting in front of one of the workstations with her arms crossed across her chest, staring at the screen. After about 15 minutes he noticed that she was still in the same position, only now she was impatiently tapping her foot. He asked if she needed help and she replied: "It's about time! I pressed the F1 button over twenty minutes ago!"

INTERNET PAYMENT

Some people pay for their online services with checks made payable to "The Internet".

INITIALIZE DISKS

An unfailingly polite lady called to ask for help with a Windows installation that had gone terribly wrong:

Customer: "I brought my Windows disks from work to install them on my home computer." Training stresses that we are "not the Software Police," so I let the little act of piracy slide.
Tech Support: "Umm-hmm. What happened?"
Customer: "As I put each disk in it turns out they weren't initialized."
Tech Support: "Do you remember the message exactly, ma'am?"
Customer: (proudly) "I wrote it down. 'This is not a Macintosh disk. Would you like to initialize it?'"
Tech Support: "Er, what happened next?"
Customer: "After they were initialized, all the disks appeared to be blank. And now I brought them back to work, and I can't read them in the A: drive; the PC wants to format them. And this is our only set of Windows disks for the whole office. Did I do something wrong?"

LUNAR LANDER

Customer: "My computer crashed!"
Tech Support: "It crashed?"
Customer: "Yeah, it won't let me play my game."
Tech Support: "All right, hit Control-Alt-Delete to reboot."
Customer: "No, it didn't crash–it crashed."

Tech Support: "Huh?"

Customer: "I crashed my game. That's what I said before. Now it doesn't work."

Turned out, the user was playing Lunar Lander and crashed his spaceship.

Tech Support: "Click on 'File,' then 'New Game.'"

Customer: [pause] "Wow! How'd you learn how to do that?"

TYPE THE LETTER "P"

Tech Support: "OK Bob, let's press the control and escape keys at the same time. That brings up a task list in the middle of the screen. Now type the letter 'P' to bring up the Program Manager."

Customer: "I don't have a 'P'."

Tech Support: "On your keyboard, Bob."

Customer: "What do you mean?"

Tech Support: "'P' on your keyboard, Bob."

Customer: "I'm not going to do that!"

THE LATEST VERSION

Customer: "So that'll get me connected to the Internet, right?"

Tech Support: "Yeah."

Customer: "And that's the latest version of the Internet, right?"

Tech Support: "Uhh...uh...uh...yeah."

Netscape Technical Support Folly

Tech: Internet Technical Support this is so-and-so speaking. May I have your username please?

Female Customer: Yes I want to speak to the person in charge immediately!

Tech: Speaking. What can I do for you?

Female Customer: I want to complain about the pornographic bookmarks your company put in my web browser!

Tech: We didn't put any pornographic bookmarks in your web browser.

Female Customer: Oh yes you did! I'm looking at them right now!
(Tech remembers the 'Netscape' history list and grins to himself)
Tech: Where exactly are these "bookmarks" located?
Female Customer: In 'Netscape'!
Tech: And where exactly in 'Netscape' would that be?
Female Customer: In that little list that comes down when you click the little down arrow!
Tech: The one right above the Net Search button?
Female Customer: Yes that one!
Tech: Miss, that's the 'Netscape' history list. Netscape keeps the past ten links you typed in that box. The only way to put an address in that box is for someone to physically sit at your computer and type in a web address.
Female Customer: Well I certainly didn't type in those X rated web addresses!
Tech: Well somebody did. Who else has access to your computer, and uses the Internet?
Female Customer: Just me and my husband!
(Several seconds of silence pass. Hey! I wasn't going to say it!)
Female Customer:…oh…OOOH!…Thank you.
(She quickly hung up)

MISCELLANEOUS

"I really love dealing with customers. To me it's like enjoying Neapolitan ice cream compared to plain vanilla since no two individuals are exactly the same or have the same needs. Dealing with different customers, requirements and idiosyncrasies makes life much more flavorful!"

Toby started Unwind.com with a vision to have an online destination that would cater to the varying individual approaches that people use to relax and unwind. "While stress-related tools and information do the trick for some, we've found that many folks can destress just as well by simply including some laughter or soothing music into their hectic days. Jokes-Funnies.com is our own homegrown, "frown-cracking" approach to making people relax through laughter. We've grown our jokes site to include 1000's of pages of content and currently are averaging more than 150,000 hits/day. That's what we call sharing some smiles!"

Toby is currently involved in many facets of the technology industry. He splits his time as President of Unwind.com (Jokes-Funnies.com, Relaxation.com, Unwind.FM and ShopUnwind.com), a partner at Burns Development Group, which is a community development company that's focused on economic development in rural areas of Mississippi and the Southern U.S., founder of Sightseer Commercial Properties (a commercial real estate and virtual tour company) and AIR2LAN, a wireless Internet broadband services provider, where Toby leads the Web Services division. Prior to joining AIR2LAN, Toby was Vice President, Internet Products Group for Business Communications, Inc. In that position he was responsible for developing and managing the Internet application and integration division. Prior to this position, Toby founded and managed award-winning software and interactive development divisions for a number of other leading companies including Modern World Multimedia and Electric Arts, Inc.

Editor's note: Toby Shenefelt has certifications in many disciplines, including Java, C++, E-Commerce Infrastructure, Certificate Management, Directory Analysis and Planning, ECXpert, and Project Management and graduated Magna Cum Laude from Berklee College of Music in Boston, MA., where his studies focused on Music Synthesis and emerging Computer Production technologies. Be sure to visit his website at http://www.unwind.com/jokes-funnies.

The following is a collection of miscellaneous jokes, poems, and all around technician fun. We love to make fun of the customers. Contributors include: Unwind, Daniel Macks, Funny2, Cubicle Commando, CompGuys and HumorShack.

Some users take their computers too seriously.

WHAT A DAY!

Dear God:
Yesterday was an awful day for me…
My husband ran off with his secretary,
My son pierced his eyebrow,
My daughter tattooed the bald spot on her head,
My dog mated with the neighbor's cat,
My neighbor sold her house to a mental institution,
My Mom told me I was adopted,
My Dad told me he's gay,
My boss told me I was laid off,
My sister was arrested for prostitution,

My house has termites,
My car was stolen,
All that came in the mail was bills,
A plane crash-landed on my garage,
OJ Simpson came to my door selling rug cleaner,
And my TV blew.
Lord, please be with me today.
I was able to live through all that misery yesterday.
And I will be able to make it through anything today! But please....
DON'T LET ANYTHING HAPPEN TO MY COMPUTER!!!!!
AMEN

Too many of us computer technicians can pass the following quiz with flying colors. This isn't one we can really pin on the customers, but who cares? If you score less than seven, send me an email. Let's have some fun!

COMPUTER GEEK QUIZ

1. I have moss growing:
A) In my garden
B) In my bathroom
C) In my kitchen
D) On my teeth

2. When I open my mouth at parties, people:
A) Listen
B) Ease away slowly
C) Stuff a live weasel down my throat

3. I think computers are:
A) Uninteresting
B) Interesting
C) Too damn small for the stuff I want to do

4. I think sheep are:
A) Uninteresting
B) Interesting
C) Annoyingly far away from where I live

5. The Usenet Oracle is:
A) pack of weenies who think about "Lisa" way too much
B) Interesting
C) Not appreciative of the great answers I write; the Priesthood is out to get me

6. The gender I desire to have sexual relations with is:
A) Difficult to understand
B) Impossible to understand
C) Clearly from a different planet
D) How should I know? I've only seen pictures

7. Bill Gates is:
A) Bill who?
B) Very wealthy
C) Head of Microsoft, which produces some widely used products
D) The Antichrist

8. In general, people:
A) Like me
B) Don't like me
C) People? What people?

9. My friends are:
A) Diverse
B) People I know from work or school
C) Wearing the same clothing I am

10. My dream vacation is:
A) Tibet

B) Europe

C) California

D) In a room with lots of fluorescent lights and an unlimited supply of coffee

11. My job prospects are:

A) Abysmal

B) Adequate

C) I'll never be out of work, you hear me? Never!

D) They pay people to do this?

Score 0 for each A, 1 for each B, 2 for each C, and 3 for each D.

19 or more: Yep. You're a computer geek, all right.

13–18: You're a geek of some stripe or another.

7–12: Probably not a geek, but watch it…

0–6: If you're of the opposite sex, could you leave a note for me in the personals column? Please? Hello?

I've never been adventurous enough to try any of these lines, but now I understand why so many computer technicians are single!

PICKUP LINES FOR COMPUTER GEEKS

—Nice Set of Floppies!

—Hey, how 'bout I take off your cover and insert a bigger CPU.

—I'd like to play on your laptop.

—Need me to unzip your files?

—If you were an ISP, I'd dial you all day long!

—I'd like to boot up your PC!

—I'll bet my hard drive is the biggest you've ever seen!

—I've got a 21-inch…(monitor)

—I'd get a T3 to watch your streaming video…

—Your homepage or mine?

YOU KNOW YOU ARE A COMPUTER ADDICT WHEN...

1: You wake up at 3:00AM to go to the bathroom and you stop and check your e-mail on the way through.
2: You get a tattoo that reads: This body best viewed with 'Internet Explorer 5.0' or better.
3: You name a child 'Explorer', 'Mozilla', or 'Outlook Express'.
4: You turn off your computer and get this empty lonely feeling like you just pulled the plug on a loved one's life support system.
5: You spend 7 hours driving around trying to find a 12 volt adapter for your laptop so going shopping will be more productive.
6: You stay in college for an additional year or two for the free Internet access.
7: You laugh at people with 28.8 modems and wonder how evolution actually occurred.
8: You start using smileycons in your responses at the other tech site (which shall remain nameless).
9: You find yourself typing com after every period when using your word processor.
10: You refer to going to the bathroom as downloading or streaming audio.
11: You start introducing yourself as johndoe@alwaysfreakingonline.net.
12: Your friends all have @ in their names.
13: Your family pet has it's own web page.
14: Your excuse for not calling your relatives is: they don't have a modem.
15: You check your e-mail, it says you have no new messages, so you check it again.
16: Your phone bill is the lowest in the neighborhood because you can't get off the computer long enough to make long distance calls.
17: When filling out applications you write your address as johndoe@alwaysfreakingonline.net, and your qualifications as your system's components.

18: You get to know your tech support agent better than your own wife.
19: You dream in 16-bit color.
20: You spend most of your honeymoon formatting your hard drive and reinstalling 'Windows'.
21: You take your laptop to the Ball Game.
22: You refer to Microsoft using an uncomplimentary name.
23: You buy your toothpaste and toilet paper online.
24: You wonder if they'll ever bring back the 'Commodore 64'.

New Computer Viruses

You can blame a lot of computer problems on viruses—and the customers are none the wiser. The trick is coming up with a believable name and definition. Beware of the following new computer viruses!

AIRLINE VIRUS
You're in Dallas, but your data is in Singapore.

AT&T VIRUS
Every three minutes it tells you what great service you are getting.

DISNEY VIRUS
Everything in the computer goes Goofy.

GOVERNMENT ECONOMIST VIRUS
Nothing works, but all your diagnostic software says everything is fine.

HOWARD STERN VIRUS
One of the dirtiest viruses around. It writes 4 letter words to all of your files just to annoy the operating system. It also installs an X-rated GIF on your hard drive. Very popular.

JEFFREY DAHMER VIRUS
Eats away at your systems resources piece by piece.

KEVORKIAN VIRUS
Helps your computer shut down whenever it wants to; as an act of mercy.

LAPD VIRUS
It claims it feels threatened by the other files on your PC and erases them in "self-defense."

LORENA BOBBITT VIRUS
It turns your hard disk into a 3.5 inch floppy.

MCI VIRUS
Every three minutes it reminds you that you're paying too much for the AT&T virus.

MIKE TYSON VIRUS
Leaves its mark on you XXX.GIF files. Quits after one byte.

O.J. SIMPSON VIRUS
It claims that it did not, could not, and would not delete two of your files and vows to find the virus that did it.

O.J. SIMPSON VIRUS #2
You know it killed your system but you just can't prove it.

OPRAH WINFREY VIRUS
Your 200MB hard drive suddenly shrinks to 80MB, and then slowly expands to 300MB.

PBS VIRUS
Your computer stops every few minutes to ask for a tax-deductible contribution.

ROSANNE BARR VIRUS
Plays the National Anthem at boot-up. Even worse with a sound card.

ROSS PEROT VIRUS #2
It activates every component in your system, just before the whole darn thing quits.

SPICE GIRL VIRUS
Has no real function, but makes a pretty desktop.

STAR TREK VIRUS
Invades your system in places where no virus has gone before.

WATERGATE VIRUS
Erases 18 minutes off your tape backup.

X-FILES VIRUS
All your icons start shape shifting.

Psychic Support 1

Support: Hello, and thank you for calling the Psychic Friends Computer Support Network! How can I help you?

Customer: Hi, I tried to open up a file, but the computer says "Cannot open A:\report.doc".

Support: Ah, this file is stored on a floppy disk, isn't it?

Customer: Wow! How could you know that?

Support: I know many, many things. For instance, this file of yours, it is some sort of report that you are working on, right? In Microsoft Word?

Customer: Unbelievable! You really are psychic! Well, how can I open this file?

Support: I see a…I see a…I see a message. It is an error message. It says, "This file is corrupted, click here for more details."

Customer: Well?

Support: Do it! You must click.

Customer: Do what?

Support: Say "Click"!

Customer: Click!

Support: No, double click! Double click!

Customer: Click Click! Click Click!

Support: Now I see another message. "In the future, do not save your only copy to a floppy disk. Save a copy on your hard drive". Ah, the vision is gone. Thank you for calling. If you stay on the line an operator will speak with you about sending your disk in for a file recovery. It is only $45 plus shipping.

THINGS YOU DON'T WANT TO HEAR FROM TECH SUPPORT

* "Do you have a sledgehammer or a brick handy?"
* "That's right, not even McGyver could fix it."
* "So—what are you wearing?"
* "Duuuuuuude! Bummer!"
* "Looks like you're gonna need some new dilithium crystals, Cap'n."
* "Press 1 for Support. Press 2 if you're with 60 Minutes. Press 3 if you're with the FTC."
* "We can fix this, but you're gonna need a butter knife, a roll of duct tape, and a car battery."
* "In layman's terms, we call that the Hindenburg Effect."
* "Hold on a second...Mom! Timmy's hitting me!"
* "Okay, turn to page 523 in your copy of Dianetics."
* "Please hold for Mr. Gates' attorney."

Top 20 Phone Tech Support No-No's

I know I've used a couple of these lines before. But this isn't about me. This is about you.

20. Try to sell homemade LSD to caller.
19. "Still not used to this whole electricity thing, huh?"
18. Proclaim your undying love.
17. Advise the customer to lick the power supply.
16. "So, what are you wearing?"
15. Constantly refer to caller as "Pumpkin".
14. As you look up a part number, whistle loudly in a monotone.
13. "You've got to be kidding."
12. "What you do is get yourself 50 cents and go and buy a clue."
11. Use baby talk.
10. "I don't get paid enough to deal with jerks like you."
9. Ridicule the inadequacy of the caller's system.

8. "Yo no hablo ingles."
7. Use metaphors based on your experiences with rabid dogs.
6. Laugh maniacally.
5. Twist the caller's words to make it seem as if there is no problem.
4. "You're screwed. You're just screwed."
3. Encourage the caller to pound on the CPU casing.
2. Try to set up caller with your second cousin.
1. "How the hell did you get access to a computer?"

TOP 10 SIGNS YOUR CO-WORKER IS A COMPUTER HACKER

I'm innocent I tell ya! I delved into the hacking world for a few months (it's addicting)…until I got caught by a friend. I inadvertently mentioned how good one of her reports for school was. She hadn't told or showed anyone anything about the report. Whoops!

10) You ticked him off once and your next phone bill was for $20,000.
9) He's won the Publisher's Clearing House sweepstakes 3 years running.
8) When asked for his phone number, he gives it in hex.
7) Seems strangely calm whenever the office LAN goes down.
6) Somehow gets HBO on his PC at work.
5) Mumbled, "Oh, puh-leeez" 95 times during the movie "The Net".
4) Massive 401k contribution made in half-cent increments.
3) His video dating profile lists "public-key encryption" among turn-ons.
2) When his computer starts up, you hear, "Good Morning, Mr. President".
1) You hear him murmur, "Let's see you use that Visa card now, Professor I-Don't-Give-A's-In-Computer-Science!"

50 ways to confuse, worry, or just scare people in the computer lab

1. Log on, wait a sec, then get a frightened look on your face and scream "Oh my God! They've found me!" and bolt.

2. Laugh uncontrollably for about 3 minutes & then suddenly stop and look suspiciously at everyone who looks at you.

3. When your computer is turned off, complain to the monitor on duty that you can't get the damn thing to work. After he/she's turned it on, wait 5 minutes, turn it off again, & repeat the process for a good half-hour.

4. Type frantically, often stopping to look at the person next to you evilly.

5. Before anyone else is in the lab, connect each computer to a different screen than the one it's set up with.

6. Write a program that plays the "Smurfs" theme song and play it at the highest volume possible over & over again.

7. Work normally for a while. Suddenly look amazingly startled by something on the screen and crawl underneath the desk.

8. Ask the person next to you if they know how to tap into top-secret Pentagon files.

9. Use Interactive Send to make passes at people you don't know.

10. Make a small ritual sacrifice to the computer before you turn it on.

11. Bring a chainsaw, but don't use it. If anyone asks why you have it, say "Just in case…" mysteriously.

12. Type on VAX for a while. Suddenly start cursing for 3 minutes at everything bad about your life. Then stop and continue typing.

13. Enter the lab, undress, and start staring at other people as if they're crazy while typing.

14. Light candles in a pentagram around your terminal before starting.

15. Ask around for a spare disk. Offer $2. Keep asking until someone agrees. Then, pull a disk out of your fly and say, "Oops, I forgot."

16. Every time you press Return and there is processing time required, pray "Ohpleaseohpleaseohpleaseohplease," and scream "YES!" when it finishes.

17. "DISK FIGHT!!!"

18. Start making out with the person at the terminal next to you (It helps if you know them, but this is also a great way to make new friends).

19. Put a straw in your mouth and put your hands in your pockets. Type by hitting the keys with the straw.
20. If you're sitting in a swivel chair, spin around singing "The Lion Sleeps Tonight" whenever there is processing time required.
21. Draw a picture of a woman (or man) on a piece of paper, tape it to your monitor. Try to seduce it. Act like it hates you and then complain loudly that women (men) are worthless.
22. Try to stick a Nintendo cartridge into the 3 1/2 disk drive. When it doesn't work, get the supervisor.
23. When you are on an IBM, and when you turn it on, ask loudly where the smiling Apple face is.
24. Print out the complete works of Shakespeare, then when its all done (two days later) say that all you wanted was one line.
25. Sit and stare at the screen, biting your nails noisily. After doing this for a while, spit them out at the feet of the person next to you.
26. Stare at the screen, grind your teeth, stop, look at the person next to you, grinding. Repeat procedure, making sure you never provoke the person enough to let them blow up, as this releases tension, and it is far more effective to let them linger.
27. If you have long hair, take a typing break, look for split ends, cut them and deposit them on your neighbor's keyboard as you leave.
28. Put a large, gold-framed portrait of the British Royal Family on your desk and loudly proclaim that it inspires you.
29. Come to the lab wearing several layers of socks. Remove shoes and place them of top of the monitor. Remove socks layer by layer and drape them around the monitor. Exclaim sudden haiku about the aesthetic beauty of cotton on plastic.
30. Take the keyboard and sit under the computer. Type up your paper like this. Then go to the lab supervisor and complain about the bad working conditions.
31. Laugh hysterically, shout "You will all perish in flames!!!" and continue working.

32. Bring some dry ice & make it look like your computer is smoking.
33. Assign a musical note to every key (i.e. the Delete key is A Flat, the B key is F sharp, etc.). Whenever you hit a key, hum its note loudly. Write an entire paper this way.
34. Attempt to eat your computer's mouse.
35. Borrow someone else's keyboard by reaching over, saying "Excuse me, mind if I borrow this for a sec?", unplugging the keyboard & taking it.
36. Bring in a bunch of magnets and have fun.
37. When doing calculations, pull out an abacus and say that sometimes the old ways are best.
38. Play Pong for hours on the most powerful computer in the lab.
39. Make a loud noise of hitting the same key over and over again until you see that your neighbor is noticing (You can hit the space bar so your fill isn't affected). Then look at your neighbor's keyboard. Hit his/her delete key several times, erasing an entire word. While you do this, ask: "Does *your* delete key work?" Shake your head, and resume hitting the space bar on your keyboard. Keep doing this until you've deleted about a page of your neighbor's document. Then, suddenly exclaim: "Well, whaddya know? I've been hitting the space bar this whole time. No wonder it wasn't deleting! Ha!" Print out your document and leave.
40. Remove your disk from the drive and hide it. Go to the lab monitor and complain that your computer ate your disk. (For special effects, put some 'Elmer's Glue' on or around the disk drive. Claim that the computer is drooling.)
41. Stare at the person's next to yours screen, look really puzzled, burst out laughing, and say "You did that?" loudly. Keep laughing, grab your stuff and leave, howling as you go.
42. Point at the screen. Chant in a made up language while making elaborate hand gestures for a minute or two. Press return or the mouse, then leap back and yell "COVEEEEERRRRRR!" peek up from under the table, walk back to the computer and say. "Oh, good. It worked this time," and calmly start to type again.

43. Keep looking at invisible bugs and trying to swat them.
44. See who's online. Send a total stranger a talk request. Talk to them like you've known them all your lives. Hang-up before they get a chance to figure out you're a total stranger.
45. Bring an small tape player with a tape of really absurd sound effects. Pretend it's the computer and look really lost.
46. Pull out a pencil. Start writing on the screen. Complain that the lead doesn't work.
47. Come into the computer lab wearing several endangered species of flowers in your hair. Smile incessantly. Type a sentence, then laugh happily, exclaim "You're such a marvel!!", and kiss the screen. Repeat this after every sentence. As your ecstasy mounts, also hug the keyboard. Finally, hug your neighbor, then the computer assistant, and walk out.
48. Run into the computer lab, shout "Armageddon is here!!!!!", then calmly sit down and begin to type.
49. Quietly walk into the computer lab with a 'Black and Decker' chainsaw, rev that baby up, and then walk up to the nearest person and say, "Give me that computer or you'll be feeding my pet crocodile for the next week".
50. Two words: Tesla Coil.

What If Dr. Seuss Wrote Technical Manuals

If a packet hits a pocket on a socket on a port,
And the bus is interrupted as a very last resort,
and the address of the memory makes your floppy disk abort,
Then the socket packet pocket has an error to report!

If your cursor finds a menu item followed by a dash,
And the double-clicking icons put your window in the trash,
And your data is corrupted 'cause the index doesn't hash,
Then your situation's hopeless, and your system's gonna crash!

If the label on your cable on the gable at your house,
Says the network is connected to the button on your mouse,
But your packets want to tunnel to another protocol,
That's repeatedly rejected by the printer down the hall.

And your screen is all distorted by the side effects of gauss,
So your icons in the window are as wavy as a souse,
Then you may as well reboot and go out with a bang,
'Cause as sure as I'm a poet, the sucker's gonna hang!

When the copy of your floppy's getting sloppy on the disk,
And the microcode instructions cause unnecessary RISC,
Then you have to flash your memory and you'll want to RAM your ROM,
Quickly turn off your computer and be sure to tell your mom!

Computer Haiku

Each only 17 syllables, in the 5 7 5 format.

A file that big?
It might be very useful.
But now it is gone.

The web site you seek
Cannot be located but
Countless more exist.

Chaos reigns within.
Reflect, repent, and reboot.
Order shall return.

Aborted effort:
Close all that you have worked on.
You ask way too much.

Windows NT crashed.
I am the blue screen of death.
No one hears your screams.

Yesterday it worked.
Today it is not working.
Windows is like that.

First snow, then silence.
This thousand-dollar screen dies
So beautifully.

With searching comes loss
And the presence of absence:
"My novel" not found.

The Tao that is seen
Is not the true Tao, until
You bring fresh toner.

Stay the patient course.
Of little worth is your ire.
The network is down.

A crash reduces
Your expensive computer
To a simple stone.

Three things are certain:
Death, taxes, and lost data.
Guess which has occurred.

You step in the stream,
But the water has moved on.
This page is not here.

Out of memory.
We wish to hold the whole sky,
But we never will.

Having been erased,
The document you're seeking
Must now be retyped.

Serious error.
All shortcuts have disappeared.
Screen. Mind. Both are blank.

Computer Spell Checkers

Eye halve a spelling chequer
It came with my pea sea
It plainly marques four my revue
Miss steaks eye kin knot sea.

Eye strike a key and type a word
And weight four it two say
Weather eye am wrong oar write
It shows me strait a weigh.

As soon as a mist ache is maid
It nose bee fore two long
And eye can put the error rite
Its rare lea ever wrong.

Eye have run this poem threw it
I am shore your pleased two no
Its letter perfect awl the weigh
My chequer tolled me sew.

Phone Callin'

By: *Daniel Macks*
Original: "Free Fallin'" (Tom Petty)

She's a good girl, just got a modem
Wants Eudora, and AOL too
She's a good girl, but she&##9;s clueless,
And her hardware's unsupported, too.
It's a long day, sittin' in 101
As the users stream in the door.
And he's a bad boy, cause he didn't make backups
Then his disk crashed—won't mount anymore.

Chorus:

And they're phone, phone callin'
Yeah, from home, phone callin'
From off campus, the users are freaking
'Cause the Ciscos have just crashed hard
And the bad boys all want more modems
While the good girls have Ethernet cards.

Repeat Chorus

I wanna glide down into the cluster
Hit The Button mounted on the wall
And I'll kick back, watch them all scatter,
Won't have to change toner at all.
Repeat Chorus & Fade

This is the end of the line folks; I get off at the next bus stop. I think this final poem sums it up for all of us computer technicians. Be good, or at least be good at it!

WORKER JED

Come and listen to a story 'bout a man named Jed,
A poor college kid, barely kept his family fed,
But then one day he was talking to a recruiter,
Who said, "they pay big bucks if ya work on a computer…"
(Windows, that is…PC's…Workstations…)

Well, the first thing ya know ol' Jed's an Engineer.
The kinfolk said "Jed, move away from here".
They said "California is the place ya oughta be",
So he bought some donuts and moved to Silicon Valley…
(Intel, that is…Pentium…big amusement park…)

On his first day at work, they stuck him in a cube.
Fed him more donuts and sat him at a tube.
They said "your project's late, but we know just what to do.
Instead of 40 hours, we'll work you 52!"
(OT, that is…unpaid…mandatory…)

The weeks rolled by and things were looking bad.
Schedules started slipping and some managers were mad.
They called another meeting and decided on a fix.
The answer was simple…"We'll work him sixty-six!"
(Tired, that is…stressed out…no social life…)

Months turned to years and his hair was turning gray.
Jed worked very hard while his life slipped away.
Waiting to retire when he turned 64,
Instead he got a call and escorted out the door.
(Laid off, that is…de-briefed…unemployed…)

Now the moral of the story is listen to what you're told,
Companies will use you and discard you when you're old.
So gather up your friends and start up your own firm,

Beat the competition, and watch the bosses squirm.
(Millionaires, that is...Bill Gates...Steve Case...)

Y'all come back now...ya hear'

About the Author

Timothy D. McLendon serves as a Level 2 computer hardware technician in a major call center environment. He is Comptia A+ and Network+ certified, currently working towards MCSA status. He can be reached by e-mail at tim_mclendon@hotmail.com.

GLOSSARY

* PCMCIA—People Can't Memorize Computer Industry Acronyms
* ISDN–It Still Does Nothing
* SCSI–System Can't See It
* DOS–Defective Operating System
* BASIC–Bill's Attempt to Seize Industry Control
* IBM–I Blame Microsoft
* DEC–Do Expect Cuts
* CD-ROM–Consumer Device, Rendered Obsolete in Months
* OS/2–Obsolete Soon, Too.
* WWW–World Wide Wait
* MACINTOSH–Most Applications Crash; If Not, The Operating System Hangs
* PENTIUM–Produces Erroneous Numbers Thru Incorrect Understanding of Mathematics
* COBOL–Completely Obsolete Business Oriented Language
* AMIGA–A Merely Insignificant Game Addiction
* LISP–Lots of Infuriating & Silly Parenthesis
* MIPS–Meaningless Indication of Processor Speed
* WINDOWS–Will Install Needless Data On Whole System
* MICROSOFT–Most Intelligent Customers Realize Our Software Only Fools Teenagers
*RISC–Reduced Into Silly Code
And more....

* BIT–A word used to describe computers, as in "Our son's computer cost quite a bit."
* BOOT–What your friends give you because you spend too much time bragging about your computer skills.
* BUG–What your eyes do after you stare at the tiny green computer screen for more than 15 minutes. Also: what computer magazine companies do to you after they get your name on their mailing list.
* CHIPS–The fattening, non-nutritional food computer users eat to avoid having to leave their keyboards for meals.
* COPY–What you have to do during school tests because you spend too much time at the computer and not enough time studying.
* CURSOR–What you turn into when you can't get your computer to perform, as in "You $#% computer!"
* DISK–What goes out in your back after bending over a computer keyboard for seven hours at a clip.
* DUMP–The place all your former hobbies wind up soon after you install your computer.
* ERROR–What you made the first time you walked into a computer showroom to "just look."
* EXPANSION UNIT–The new room you have to build on to your home to house your computer and all its peripherals.
* FILE–What your secretary can now do to her nails six and a half hours a day, now that the computer does her day's work in 30 minutes.
* FLOPPY–The condition of a constant computer user's stomach due to lack of exercise and a steady diet of junk food (see Chips).
* HARDWARE–Tools, such as lawnmowers, rakes and other heavy equipment you haven't laid a finger on since getting your computer.
* IBM–The kind of missile your family members and friends would like to drop on your computer so you'll pay attention to them again.
* MENU–What you'll never see again after buying a computer because you'll be too poor to eat in a restaurant.

* MONITOR–Often thought to be a word associated with computers, this word actually refers to those obnoxious kids who always want to see your hall pass at school.
* PROGRAMS–Those things you used to look at on your television before you hooked your computer up to it.
* RETURN–What lots of people do with their computers after only a week and a half.
* TERMINAL–A place where you can find buses, trains and really good deals on hot computers.
* WINDOW–What you heave the computer out of after you accidentally erase a program that took you three days to set up.

0-595-23689-8

59541176R00094

Made in the USA
Lexington, KY
08 January 2017